KENYATTA'S STONE

Joslyn Gaines Vanderpool

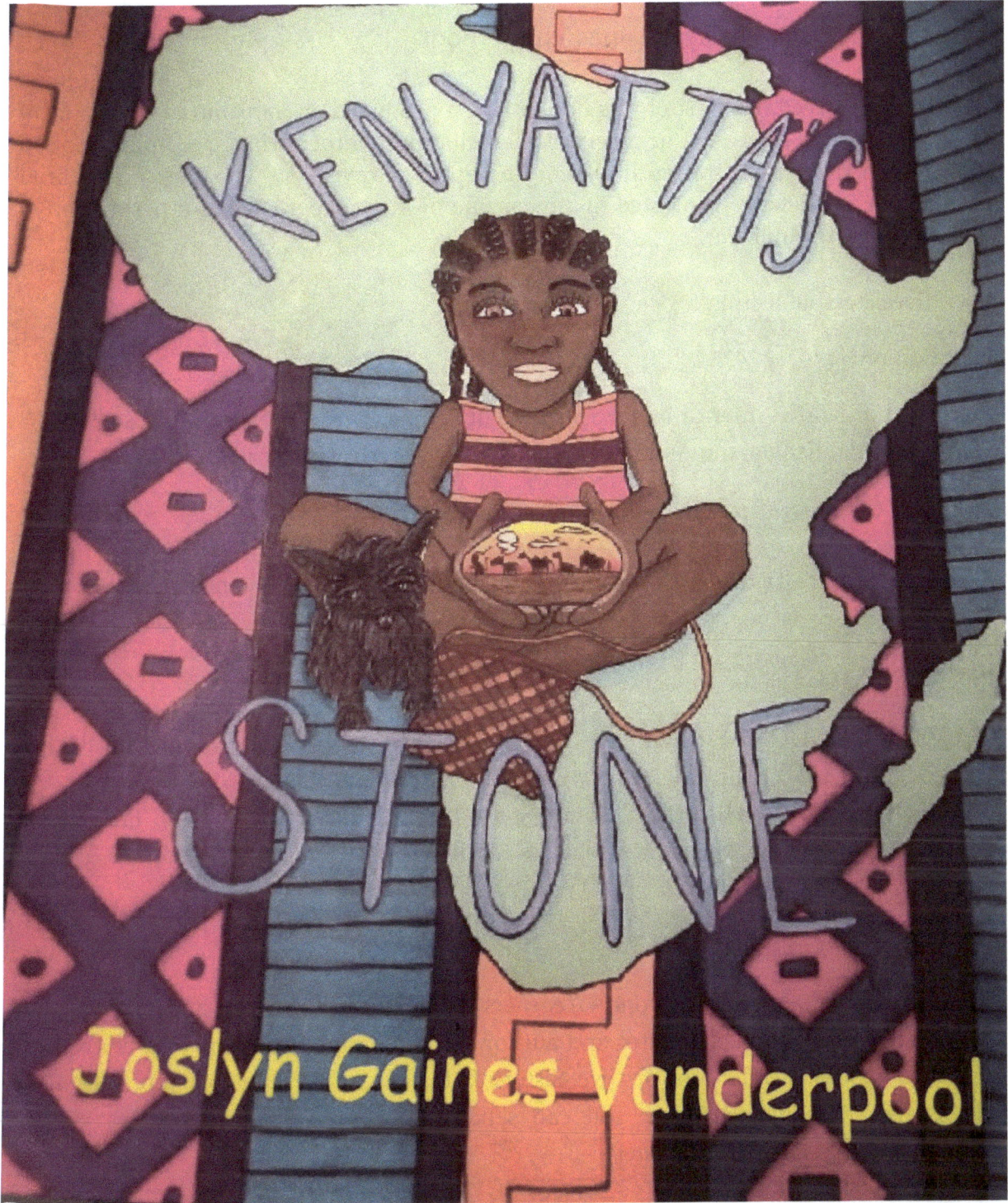

TEACHERS' COMPANION GUIDEBOOK

www.fivesisterspublishing.com

First Edition: January 2022

Published in North America by Five Sisters Publishing. For information, please contact Five Sisters Publishing, c/o Anita Royston, P.O. Box 217, Gretna, Virginia, 24557.

Library of Congress Cataloguing-In-Publication Data   2013952224

Kenyatta's Stone – Teachers' Companion Guidebook/Joslyn Gaines Vanderpool – 1st ed

ISBN: 978-1-941859-88-9

1. JUVENILE FICTION / Biographical / Africa. 2. JUVENILE FICTION / Biographical / United States. 3. JUVENILE FICTION / Diversity & Multicultural.
4. JUVENILE FICTION Historical / United States / 19th Century. 5. JUVENILE FICTION / United States / African American & Black. 6. EDUCATION / Teaching / Materials & Devices.

10   9   8   7   6   5   4   3   2   1

Comments about *Kenyatta's Stone – Teachers' Companion Guidebook* and requests for additional copies, book club rates and author speaking appearances may be addressed to Joslyn Gaines Vanderpool or Five Sisters Publishing c/o Anita Royston, P.O. Box 217, Gretna, Virginia, 24557, or you can send your comments and requests via e-mail to joslyngaines@comcast.net

Also available as an eBook from Internet retailers and from Five Sisters Publishing

Printed in the United States of America

TEACHER'S COMPANION GUIDEBOOK

By

Joslyn Gaines Vanderpool

Preface

My great great grandparents were enslaved for nearly two decades, a fact which causes a wave of grief to wash over me that has never gone away. For many in the African American community, it is rare to know anything about our histories due to marginalization, (no records that we existed). Being enslaved was like being erased from the human race. I am grateful to know the names of those who have gone before me, and humbled about what my ancestors, gave, and endured for me to be free to keep their legacies of resilience alive!

Kenyatta's Stone—A Bridge for Younger Students

When writing Kenyatta's Stone, I hadn't heard about children who were enslaved, but I thought that if I had been born 100 years earlier, I would have most likely been born into the institution of slavery, which was surreal. I wondered what thoughts and fears did enslaved children have? What, if any dreams, could they allow themselves to dream?

Kenyatta's Stone is a fictional work based on a true historical event that was written to help younger students learn about a large part of American History that is difficult to talk about and explain, but important to know. She is a bridge for starting the conversation about slavery. Speaking in simple but powerful terms, Kenyatta expresses her determination in returning to her homeland where she was free. With first-hand knowledge about enslavement, she relays what it is like to be owned by others, separated from her family, and treated harshly due to the color of her skin. She reveals her sadness, and fears, but her courage and bravery emerge, as does her voice and desires to see all enslaved people free and reunited with their loved ones.

*Note: Kenyatta mattered, and she deserved freedom. The voice of an enslaved child is heard and elevated. Kenyatta's story has an outcome that was unlikely for millions of the enslaved who lived their entire lives, never knowing or experiencing freedom. Thus true narratives of the enslaved that are suited for younger readers should also be incorporated in lessons plans to show that slavery was real, and while some enslaved escaped, many did not. A few narratives for children can be found in the *Resource* section of this guidebook.

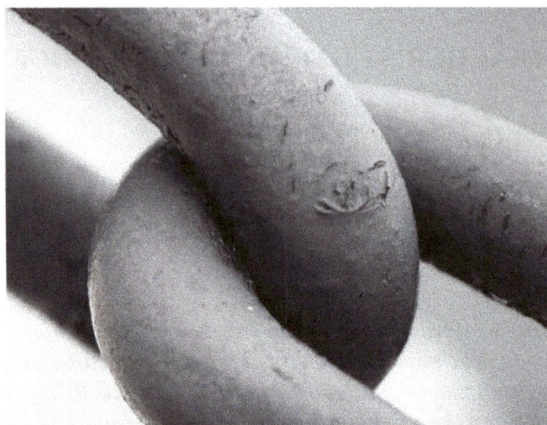

About Enslavement in America

Slavery has been a part of many societies, cultures, and countries. It is also a major, painful part of American History. Despite the fact that this Nation was established on principles that included *freedom, justice and the pursuit of happiness,* these principles were not applicable to the enslaved. In fact, slavery was legally protected by the United States Constitution. To their enslavers, people of African descent were not seen as equals and not granted citizenship until passage of the 14th Amendment. For more than two centuries, millions of people of African descent toiled their lives away under inhumane and oppressive conditions, forced into servitude to build the U.S. economy.

The enslaved had no ownership of their lives, or bodies, and no dreams or hopes to speak of. Their experiences, achievements, and contributions, before, during and after slavery have been largely absent from the American History narrative. Such an omission has led to misconceptions, inaccuracies, and pain for those whose visibility and value has been either misconstrued, forgotten or erased. As a subject in the classroom and in general, the saga of enslavement has not been fully exposed or explored for what it has done to those who endured the institution of slavery, and those who are left to contend with its legacy.

Why is Teaching about Slavery Relevant Today?

Although the enslavement of people of African descent ended more than a century and a half ago in America, some of the aftereffects of the oppressive institution linger, despite many gains made through decades of advocacy by the National Association for the Advancement of Colored People (NAACP), the passage of Civil Rights legislation in the 1950s and 1960s and the protests and marches of today, especially related to police inflicted crimes against Black people. Some of the very serious issues relating to race that plague today's society are rooted in slavery and the racism it was founded on, but by beginning a dialogue and sharing a history that has been hidden, change is possible.

With the concepts of inclusiveness and transparency that are commonly mentioned today, the time is overdue to make the connections between the past and present and delve into addressing Black History, which is American History. It is critical to begin solving a puzzle that cannot be completed until all the pieces, which are the stories of people of African descent who participated in the making of America, are included. The same holds true for other oppressed groups whose histories and contributions have not been revealed as part of America's rich historical legacy.

On June 21, 2021, more than 150 years after slavery ended, Juneteenth, has finally been recognized as an official United States federal holiday.

Freedom Day in the New Millennium

When President Abraham Lincoln signed the Emancipation Proclamation on January 1, 1863, many enslaved African Americans in America were freed. However, there were still more than 250,000 thousand enslaved people of African descent in Texas who were not notified about their freedom until June 19, 1865. In the following year, the first Juneteenth Day, was established in Galveston, Texas, and has since been celebrated in African American communities, as "Freedom Day" throughout the United States.

African American Contributions

People of African descent have enriched the global landscape in myriad ways through culture, traditions, creativity, resilience and innovation. Besides having the "longest human history" of any of the other continents, they also led the way for the first medicinal discoveries, created the first civilization in ancient Egypt and built empires in Nigeria and other countries in Africa.

Despite years of oppression, people of African descent continue to play a crucial role in every aspect of life. When they were enslaved, their gifts and talents in agricultural science, crafts, and architecture were exploited to build structures like the White House and the United States Capital, as well as universities and plantations. In addition, their knowledge of cultivating crops and farming, in addition to providing forced, free labor helped establish America's booming economy.

For centuries, and even now, people of African descent have had to fight for justice, peace, and equality. In the face of adversity, including denial of basic human rights and physical violence, they have created a blueprint that many other oppressed groups have adopted throughout the decades of striving to garner civil rights through protests, prayers, marches, demonstrations, and advocacy.

Source: diyanu.com; "International Day for People of African Descent," un.org.

OVERVIEW OF THE TEACHER'S COMPANION GUIDEBOOK

This Teacher's Companion Guidebook is designed for teachers to use for further review of *Kenyatta's Stone*, and other related subject matter pertaining to African and African American History before, after and during the saga of slavery in America. It is in no way a complete history or standalone source, but a way to start discussions with youth. Please feel free to determine what materials work best for your lesson plans and the age of your students.

Please note that all the quizzes/activities, the **List of Websites Hand-Out, Terms to Know, Kenyatta's Assignment,** *and* **Word Lists** *can be copied for students. Some activities can be adapted, based on the age and maturity of student(s). The following provides a brief explanation of how to use the materials in the guidebook:*

1. **BEFORE BEGINNING — KEYS TO EMPOWERED TEACHING AND LEARNING**
    Provides steps to starting the lessons and how and where to begin. Please see the *Resource* section for an overview for teachers. Also see https://www.rebekahgienapp.com/talk-with-children-about-slavery/.

2. **OBJECTIVES, STUDENT LEARNING OUTCOMES, SAMPLE LESSON TOPICS**

3. **QUIZZES/ACTIVITIES (Information for Teachers)** — This section explains how you can use the quiz/activity hand-outs in different ways. Answer keys are provided near the end of the guidebook. Some exercises are just for free thought and discussion. Feel free to share, duplicate and use the quizzes and activities hand-outs and other materials in the Student's Corner for your students. To save paper, instructors might consider printing front to back copies of materials that are more than one page.

4. **LIST OF WEBSITES HAND-OUT** — This sheet provides a compilation of websites that the teacher and students can use that will be helpful in finding answers to some of the questions in various sections of the guidebook. *Kenyatta's Stone* can also be used for several of the quizzes and discussions.

5. **TIMELINE OF AFRICAN AMERICAN HISTORY** — Please review the following websites regarding the timeline and use as a reference: ducksters.com, kids.britannica.com; Monet Henricks, "African American Timeline," socialstudies.com; YouTube *History of African Americans* (video).

6. **VILLAGE CIRCLE DISCUSSIONS (Free Thought Questions)** — Provides topics and questions to allow students (depending on age) an opportunity to ask questions, share feelings and emotions and respond to questions read by the teacher.

7. **Overview: Enslavement in America and Life After the Civil War... What Do You Know?** — Allows students to learn about the subject on a deeper level. There is an overview and answers at the end of this guidebook for teachers, but the subject is broad so more resources can be tapped such as the short videos that are listed in the *Resource* section and the websites provided on the *List of Websites* handout.

8. **PROJECT IDEAS AND SUGGESTIONS** — Presents ideas that the teacher can incorporate to enhance learning. Some of the books in the *Resource* section might be beneficial in creating projects or working on suggested projects.

9. **RESOURCE SECTION** — Provides a number of books, videos, documentaries, movies, articles, and websites to enhance the learning experience. You will find sites in the *Resource* section include sites that have worksheets and planning tools.
Important Note: Not all resources will be age appropriate, so please review everything in advance. There is a Materials section within the Resource section that is designed specifically for you, the teacher. It has more advanced information about subjects to help in your preparation.

10. **TERMS TO KNOW** — Gives students an opportunity to find out what words mean that relate to the African and African American experience.

11. **OVERVIEW OF ENSLAVEMENT IN AMERICA AND LIFE AFTER SLAVERY — WHAT DO YOU KNOW?** Research/Review and Discussion

12. **ANSWER KEY** — For teachers use to check answers.

13. **TIMELINE: SLAVERY THROUGH CIVIL RIGHTS MOVEMENT AND BEYOND** — This is an abbreviated history from the first enslavement of Africans in America until some present-day history is included as a summation. For more timelines, see list of websites: ducksters.com, kids.britannica.com; Monet Henricks, African American Timeline, socialstudies.com; *YouTube History of African Americans* (video).

Before Beginning —
Keys to Empowering, Learning and Teaching
(Objectives Learning Outcomes, Key Takeaways, Sample Lesson Topics)

When discussing the history of Africans and African Americans, there is a timeline that began before the advent of slavery and has continued during and after slavery. **Before beginning to discuss the subject of slavery with students, it is important to spend some time providing an overview of the history, achievements, accomplishments, and other contributions and stories about Africans, and African Americans in American and World History**.

➢ Review the Resource section of this guidebook for more information on materials to help you in this important quest. Also take a look at *Teaching for Justice* and *Southern Poverty Law Center* websites and https://www.rebekahgienapp.com/talk-with-children-about-slavery/ for teaching about tolerance, racism, and the subject of slavery to school age children. This is a difficult subject that must be handled with sensitivity, and care, particularly when it comes to African American children, and younger children.

➢ *Create a village*. Learning together as a class and/or in smaller groups or circles where everyone is involved, is significant in African culture. Working together and interactive learning allows the student to be included, valued and heard.

➢ Spend time teaching about Africa and its regions, as well as its kings and queens, and dynasties to give students an opportunity to learn that people of African descent have contributed vastly to World History, and they have a rich and strong culture.

➢ Consider seeking out those in the community, (educators, scholars, historians, community members), with insight about African and African American history to create the optimum learning experience for your students.

➢ Empower your students by believing in his/her/their abilities and consider your impact on their lives and their lives on yours. This is a special time to see your students evolve and take away knowledge that might empower them to rise to their greatest potential and help create a better world.

➤ Please do not implement any type of slave reenactments, or simulations in your lessons, (such as making chains, auction blocks or replicas of slave ships, or allowing students to participate as the enslaved, and/or masters), which are very harmful to a child's psyche, which I can attest to. I grew up in the early sixties as the only Black girl in all my classes from kindergarten until 5th grade. Several of my teachers added to my suffering by treating me as an anomaly. Being ostracized, stared at, and called numerous racial epithets daily by other students was painful and had a sobering impact that affected my esteem and development until my parents intervened.

➤ Remember your own childhood dreams, fears, and challenges and allow yourself to go to places in your heart and your humanity as you teach this difficult, but critical subject.

➤ Feel free to pick and choose which quizzes and activities are right for your students or adjust how you use the information based on the grade and maturity level of your students. The quizzes or activities can be read aloud by you, the teacher, or even by students. Thereafter, the class can answer and discuss together.

➤ Introduce students to people of African descent and their various roles and professions. Expose your students to some of the traditions and contributions that are a part of our society that came from African and African American culture. Share how the enslaved resisted being in captivity to give students a more well-rounded understanding of the resilience of people of African descent. (see *Projects*, *List of Websites* Hand-out, and *Resource* sections of guide for ideas, suggestions, books, videos, articles)

➤ Along with Kenyatta's story, review real narratives of the enslaved young people, like those of Sojourner Truth, Frederick Douglass, Harriet Tubman and lesser-known individuals whose narratives are written for youth (see *Resource* section and *List of Websites* hand-out). These will provide true perspectives from the enslaved about their journey.

➤ Check out videos on **kids.brtannica.com** regarding the subject of *African Americans at a Glance* and the list of short videos that are in the *Resource* section. Other resources will be included throughout this guidebook, such as A *Timeline of Slavery through the Civil Rights Movement and Beyond*, which is an abbreviated version at the end of the guide. The *African American History Timeline*, **kids.britannica.com;** *and A Timeline of African American History in the United States* by Monet Hendricks on socialstudies.com are also very good resources and can be found online. They might also be helpful for you to review to gain a broader list of historical events.

➤ You are capable of making a difference in the lives of your students that will help empower them to become conscientious and well-informed citizens of the world. Thank you for what you do.

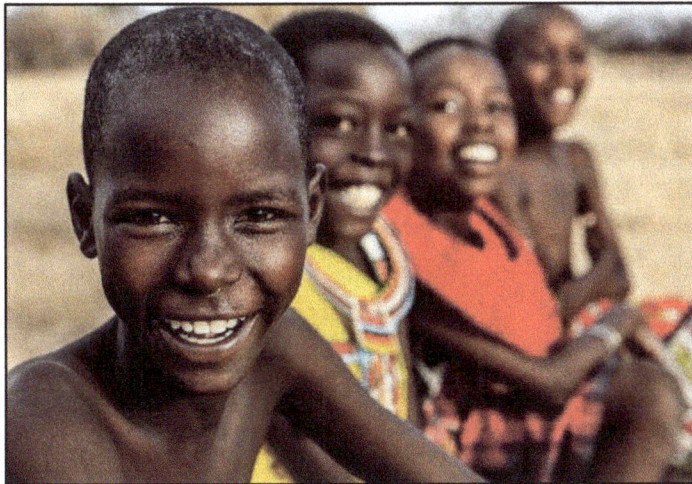

Objective — The subject of slavery is multifaceted and played a significant role in the formation of the America. Learning about the treatment of people of African descent, and about how and why slavery happened, including its impact on generations that have followed, is United States History. Therefore, the objective is to sensitively expose younger students to this difficult history to bring clarity, knowledge and truth about the lives of people of African descent and the components, conditions and consequences of enslavement.

Student Learning Outcomes—

✓ Students will be exposed to a learning model that is interactive, inclusive, and entails working together to create an optimum classroom experience.

✓ Students will discover information regarding a history that has not been widely taught; and learn about the connection between how history of the past, links to present day events.

✓ Students will be given the opportunity to share their feelings and ask questions about a difficult subject. Older students will gain opportunities to formulate and discuss their thoughts openly and begin to develop critical analytical and research skills.

Key Takeaways—

✓ Learning about slavery is a fundamental part of American history. The lessons are not designed to create fear, assign blame nor place guilt on what happened in the past. However, it is an opportunity to present true historical events that are critical to the American narrative.

✓ Learning about diverse histories, cultures and stories is critical to improving understanding, healing, and growth as a global society because the promotion of humanity, inclusion, and the importance of equality is being honestly and positively broached in a way that is relatable to youth.

✓ Questions about skin color, race, equality, and racism can be addressed openly and honestly to break through barriers that create harmful misconceptions and stereotypes.

✓ A child's voice, feelings, and perspectives are important and valuable, and should be included in conversations that deal with issues that will impact them and the world they live in.

SAMPLE LESSON TOPICS—

Lesson topics are designed to assist the teacher in planning by sharing ideas on how to approach a broad subject with many interlinking components, including race, racism, skin color, justice, equality, enslavement, and the resilience of people of African descent throughout time. Each component is important to developing a full picture of history that youth can grasp.

The topics below are merely suggestions that are placed in a specific order to build up to the topic of slavery, which should not be thrust on students without preparation. The point is to show that there are multiple layers to the history of people of African descent that should be examined, and it started in Africa. As the teacher, you know your students and their learning styles, as well as what they can handle. Based on those factors, you should be able to develop an effective lesson plan.

Consider integrating ideas from the *Projects* section, and *Free Thought Discussion* Questions, in addition to using *Kenyatta's Stone* and other books and videos that are in the *Resource* section for your lesson plans.

➢ Lesson Topic #1 — **Africa Overview.** Check out https://www.kids-world-travel-guide.com (Africa) for good information about the second-largest continent. Also read books and articles or show videos to students about the continent of Africa. Talk about the seven continents so that students have a reference point. Allow students to create a classroom chart or their own personal charts to find out about how each continent ranks in land-mass size and population. Ask about Africa's most famous landmarks and about what makes Africa unique.

➢ Lesson Topic #2— **Create a Map of Africa.** Have each student draw or you can print an image of the continent of Africa from websites that allow it, for teaching purposes. Make additional copies for your students. Please see the *Project* section for websites that have map printouts). After drawing or printing up maps and having students color them, they will be ready to start their regional studies of Africa.

➤ Lesson Topic #3 — **Researching Regions of Africa and Report Writing.** You might choose 5-10 countries in Africa to focus on such as, Egypt, Ghana, Sierra Leone, Liberia, Nigeria, the Ivory Coast and others. The West and Central coast of Africa experienced much of the slave trade in the Americas so you might include them in this assignment as it might be relatable to *Kenyatta's Stone*.

  o Choose one or two countries a week or month to explore. Older students can pretend to be travel journalists who gather information and report back to the class about one or two regions that were assigned to them. Then students can add the country they have studied to the correct location on their maps.

➤ Lesson Topic #4 — **Create a Flag of Each Country that is Included for Study.** Students can make a flag for each country they review using paper, crayons, or markers. After the flags are complete, they can be added around the classroom with information about the country, population, what the country is known for, landmarks, terrain, type of weather, language, type of homes, etc. Another option is for students to create a booklet with each country in alphabetical order, with a flag and the demographics about each place. See the *Project* section for ideas and websites like ducksters.com.

➤ Lesson Topic #5 — **Creating Crafts and Learning about African Culture.** This might entail learning about how certain structures were built and constructing a replica with cardboard or construction paper to create the Pyramids. Creations could include an item such as an important instrument, or learn about Kente cloth, art and mask making, writing up recipes to learn about region, etc. Each project should include a discussion about the meaning of item and its importance. Please see the *Project* section.

➤ Lesson Topic #6 — **Learn about the People of Africa.** Students can study about the people of Ghana, Nigeria, Mali, Egypt, South Africa, and other countries. The objective is to find out about the culture, families, traditions, foods, and the type of houses people live or lived in. Other areas to examine could be educational systems, industries, and languages spoken. Nelson Mandela was very prominent in South Africa and globally. His story could be examined and other African people of note, like Bishop Desmond Tutu.

➤ Lesson Topic #7 — **People of African Descent Contributions to the World.** Consider using Quiz #1 notable people for the aforementioned section of the guide and review books about African kings and queens, innovators, and other occupational fields that people of African descent were a part of. Some information can be found in the *Resource* guide and the *List of Websites* Hand-out regarding "African American Lists".

➤ Lesson Topic #8 — **Slave Trade from Africa to America.** Students can find out where the enslaved came from and where those countries are located on their maps. They can also determine the distance between were the enslaved were taken from to where they arrived in America, to give students a sense of the arduous, journey aboard cramped and diseased slave ships.

➤ Lesson Topic #9 — **Introduction to *Kenyatta's Stone*. Read and review *Kenyatta's Stone*,** which can take a few days or weeks to read, and complete some of the quizzes/activities. When Kenyatta asks Nana Tala, "Why do they chain up people whose skin is like ours? What have we done?" this may be good time to begin discussions about skin color and race in simple terms. See books in the *Resource* section on discussing skin color and racism to elementary age students.

➢ Lesson Topic #10 — **Free Thought Discussions.** This section of questions focuses on Kenyatta's plight and other issues about slavery and can be integrated throughout all of your lesson planning, as well as the other activities in the *Terms to Know, Overview of Enslavement in America and Beyond* and the *Projects* sections.

QUIZZES/ACTIVITIES –NOTES/INSTRUCTIONS FOR TEACHERS' USE

?

Bonus Quiz—Students have an opportunity to review the worksheet that is provided in the *Student Corner* section and to identify which pictured items might or might not have been created by African and/or African American innovators. After making their selections, students can do a research assignment looking up the names at the bottom of the page to determine who invented what. Teachers can read about the different innovators to younger children and make flash cards together with an item on one side and a name of who invented the item on the back of the card.

Quiz/Activity# 1— Notable African/African Americans in History (Look It Up!)

✓ **Where to search for answers for the following assignment:** *List of Websites Hand-out.* A notable figures' name can be typed into the search engine of **wikipedia.org** or use **kids.britannica.com**, which provides video clips and biographies on some of the individuals. It is a great tool to use in the classroom. Other websites that are child-friendly are listed on the *List of Websites* hand-out, which is included in this guidebook.

✓ This assignment is designed for older students to begin learning about the histories of a few African and African Americans, but can be adapted to work for younger students, (such as, studying one notable figure at a time, making flash cards as a class, reading about the notable individuals together, watching video clips about some of the individuals.

✓ Break down this assignment by creating teams that are comprised of 3-6 students per team depending on your class size. You can determine the number of teams and how many students will be on each team.

✓ Each team is given 5-6 individuals listed on the *Notable African/African Americans* quiz/activity sheet to learn about. Team one, for example, can research all the notable figures from A-E, which are Frederick Douglass, Martin Luther King, Jr., Sojourner Truth, Phillis Wheatly and Dred Scott. Team two would research notable figures listed from F-J, and the next team, would review K-O, etc. If there are a few individuals on the list of 26 notable figures that have not been covered by a team, then all teams should be assigned to learn about that additional person or person(s).

✓ The teacher or teams can find pictures of the individuals listed by searching online and make flash cards by pasting pictures on one side of an index card and writing up biographies on the back of the card. Another option is for each team to write up a report.

✓ After students have completed their assignment, they should be able to quiz each other, exchange the flashcards they've made with another team and should be successful in completing and answering the entire quiz/activity. An Answer Key is in the back of this guidebook for the teacher.

Quiz/Activity # 2 – Who Said or Did It? (Chapters: 1, 2, 3, 4)—This activity can be presented in chapter sections each week or month, etc. Older students can answer the questions on their own or work as a team and do an open book assignment (optional) using *Kenyatta's Stone* or be quizzed on what they remembered from the story. Younger students can read the story and answer questions as a group.

Quiz/Activity #3 – African Terms — Matching the English word with African terms is the main assignment. The words are used throughout the book, but the definition of the terms can be found on pages 3 and 16 of *Kenyatta's Stone*.

Quiz/Activity #4 – English to African Paragraph — Students have the option of using the book, *Kenyatta's Stone*, (pages 3 and 16), to rewrite a paragraph that is provided using African terms that are underlined and highlighted. Team or individual activity.

Quiz/Activity #5 — Name Where it Happened: Africa or America — Activity can be a village circle, done individually, read aloud by students or by the teacher depending on age of students and reading skill level.

Quiz/Activity #6 Multiple Choice — Can be done individually, in a village circle, or read by teacher or students.

Quiz/Activity #7 True or False with Explanations — This activity is good for group discussions, and village circles, particularly for older students. It also can be done individually as a quiz and then discussed as a group. For younger children, teacher can read aloud and allow students to respond.

Quiz/Activity #8 Word Scramble — Geared toward older students (Interactive).

✓ Allow students to form a few teams to work together to unscramble words that relate to the book, *Kenyatta's Stone*. Teams should be far enough away from each other to keep the other team from hearing their answers.

✓ All students should have pencils and a hand-out of the words that are turned face down so no one will see the words until you, the teacher, says, "Go!" At that point team members can flip over their hand-outs and work on their sheets together to unscramble the words. Although all students can write the words on their worksheets, one person per group, should be charged with being the spokesperson for the group and writing down the answers that the team has provided to share with the class. Give students about 15-20 minutes to try to unscramble 10 words.

✓ When five minutes are left, ask the teams if they are done. If they need a little more time, you can decide to grant extra time. Or you can opt to set a shorter time if you want. If there is a team that finishes first, within or before the allotted time, allow that team to give the answers.

✓ If no team, has indicated that they are done, and the allotted time has run out, you can say, "Times Up!" Afterwards allow students to say the words that they did figure out aloud. Then give the correct words that they might not have figured out. Students should be prepared to discuss how each word related to Kenyatta's story and/or enslavement.

Quiz/Activity #9 Word List for Younger Students (Handout) – Can be used for spelling tests.

Quiz/Activity #10 Random Word Lists Worksheet — Younger students can practice learning how to spell the words from their study list that go with various icons on their worksheets.

Quiz/Activity #11 Word Lists Handout (Older Students) — This list of words will help students in their studies. They should know how to spell the words and give their meanings. Students can focus on 5-10 words at a time.

Quiz/Activity #12 Word Scramble and Sentences (1-4) — Younger students can use a large, magnetized board with letters that can be placed in front of the class and then unscramble letters as a class. As another option, students can make their own letters, cut them out and paste onto index cards. Working together should be encouraged. Students can use the index cards they have made to find the letters for each word.

Free Thought Discussions — Free Thought is a great way to have meaningful discussions about the topics that are being studied. Both teacher and students form a circle to create a more inviting learning environment. Thereafter, all students can be given a chance to answer and ask questions from the talking points sheet that the teacher has. Visitors who understand the subject matter, can also be invited to participate. Students can share their feelings, exercise their curiosity, probe, learn, assess, and ask their own questions. As a class you can have discussions that cover a few questions at each session over time. Students can also express their feelings through art projects.

Tip: Before going to the *Free Thought Discussions* activities with your students, you as the teacher, might consider going to the *Projects* section of this guidebook and assigning the Declaration of Independence project, which is one of the first topics on the Free Thought Discussions talking points list. This might help students prepare beforehand.

Kenyatta Assignment — Kenyatta's trek back to Africa, seems nearly impossible, but students' get a chance to assess whether it could have been possible. This assignment will require examination of real-life people of African descent who sought to get back to their homeland. More instruction is included on the handout.

Overview: Enslavement in America after the Civil War –What Do You Know? This is a vast subject spanning more than two centuries in the United States. Slavery in America has an undeniable link to many of societies current racial issues. There are answers and notes for the teacher to review about enslavement in anticipation of students' questions in the Answer Key section of the guidebook under the title, "Overview: Enslavement in America after the Civil War".

Ask questions of older students and allow them to conduct their own research using the following to help: List of Websites Hand-out in this guidebook and sources such as kids-britannica.com; and viewing the videos *African Americans at a Glance;* and a brief *Underground Railroad: Crash Course Black American History,* YouTube video. There are pictures and biographies of many of the notable African American figures listed in quiz/activities # 1 on the **kidsbritannica.com** website. Review the *Resource* section for books and short videos. As the teacher, for your own preparation you might consider viewing *Africans in America,* **pbs.org** and *the History of Slavery in America,* YouTube, parts 1-3.

Terms to Know — Students can form a team/village or work individually to find out what terms and concepts mean that pertain to the era of enslavement and afterward. Students can type a question into Google to find potential answers. Additionally they can use the List of Websites handout and visit kidsbrittanica.com Ask questions of students and allow older students to conduct their own research or use the following to help: Consider using kids-britannica.com, *African Americans at a Glance* and reviewing the brief *Underground Railroad* video. There are pictures, biographies, and brief videos of some of the notable African American figures that were listed in Quiz/Activity # 1 in this guidebook that can be found on the kidsbrittanica.com website and on more places to search are included on the List of Websites handout.

Project Ideas

The following are ideas and suggestions. Choose projects that are age-appropriate for your students, which will add to their understanding about the seriousness and pain of enslavement and the importance of knowing that African and African American History is also American History. **Enslaved reenactments of any kind <u>should not</u> be done because they will bring harm and are extremely insensitive.** Peruse the *Resource* section for books and videos that you can review that might tie into the projects.

➢ Students can draw or trace the continent of Africa, or you, the teacher can make copies of pictures of Africa for younger children. See information about free printout maps below. Then identify where the regions listed are located on the map of Africa. **What are some of the regions where the enslaved came from?** (Mostly from West Central Africa: Angola, Benin, Cameroon, Congo, Cote d'Ivoire (or Ivory Coast in English), Gabon, Gambia, Ghana, Guinea, Mali, Nigeria, Senegal and more. Create a flag of each country listed and include Liberia, Egypt, and South Africa). Write 3-5 things about the country. **Websites:** Go to **ducksters.com,** click on Geography and then African Nations which includes flags of each country and a brief history. **Africa Blank Maps for free: allfreeprintable.com; printableworldmap.net**

➢ Find out about African and African American kings, queens, inventors, mathematicians, and scientists. Create projects from the lessons learned such as conducting experiments, or inventions, of African and African American figures in history. **Book: Africa's Little Kings and Queens by Kunda Kids. Ancient Africa, ducksters.com; African Kingdoms and Empires, kidsbritannica.com; 11 Famous African American Mathematicians You Should Know About, mashupmath.com**

➢ Draw or have students draw or print-out a United States map, and identify which states were slave and free states in 1860 or earlier through color coding which states allowed slavery, and which were free. For example students can color free states green and enslavement states blue or whatever they choose. **Free printable United States maps https://waterproofpaper.com; mapsofusa.net**

➢ Create the **Declaration of Independence** and put the following on white or beige paper, "We hold these truths to be self-evident that all men are created equal, that they are endowed by their Creator with certain inalienable Rights, that among these are Life, Liberty and the Pursuit of Happiness," and paste to black construction paper. In this lesson, help students understand the following: What does, "We hold these truths to be self-evident mean?" and review each principle of Life, Liberty, and the Pursuit of Happiness. Which ideal means freedom?

➢ **Showing Our Humanity Projects:** The class can decide which projects they can do in the community to help others, and show they care. It can be cleaning up a community park, singing a song virtually to senior citizens that they learned in class, or collecting socks or food items for the unhoused or food bank. They can also create artworks for the library or other agencies. As another option, your students can Zoom with other students who are from another part of the country or region in the world, to promote a partnership of diversity, after learning about that country and sharing good wishes. In addition, or as an alternative, students can create simple gifts for another group of students from another region of the world, or within your country or another part of your city or town.

➢ **Freedom Butterflies:** Butterflies are considered free! They are beautiful, *elusive, and *resilient and are also a sign of hope. Start a discussion about how being able to move and go where you want is symbolic of butterflies and the freedom Kenyatta and so many others sought and fought to be. Have students take paint stirring sticks or craft sticks and glue on construction paper that has been shaped like wings and decorated by students in any way they want, with paint, crayons, glitter, etc. When waved, the wings should flap. Go outside and have students wave their butterflies freely in remembrance of Kenyatta and others who were enslaved or who may not be experiencing freedom in different regions of the world. Ask students to find out what the words with the asterisk in front of them mean.

> **Courage Badge**— Kenyatta was brave because she had to deal with being enslaved every day. Younger students can create paper badges of bravery and decorate or color them as they desire. Afterward each student can explain how they have been courageous or brave in some way, (such as helping someone like parents, guardians, friends or being kind to a classmate, or trying something new, etc.) Students can also give each other a badge for courage, kindness and/or bravery.

> **Sameness/Difference Experiment**— Give students a card with the word "Me" on it. Then read aloud the questions that are listed below or questions of your own design, one at a time. If students agree it applies to them, they will raise their card in the air. Then you, or a student you designate, can do a quick count of cards in the air, and put down the tally for each question. At the end of the exercise, you or a student can announce the count of each question. The experiment will show how many similarities people have that unify us. Then you can explain how difference is also positive because we can learn about one another and appreciate what each person has to offer.

> **Sample Questions**: You, as the teacher, can ask the whole class a few or all questions or add additional questions that would prove the theory that we all have similarities, as well as differences.
1.   How many of you like bugs?
2.   How many of you have a sister or sisters?
3.   How many of you have a brother or brothers?
4.   How many of you have visited another state or country?
5.   How many of you like doing chores?
6.   How many of you like recess?
7.   How many of you like the color red?
8.   How many of you like dogs?
9.   How many of you like broccoli?
10.   How many of you like pizza?
11.   How many of you like cats?
12.   How many of you like homework?
13.   How many of you have played in the snow?
14.   How many of you like to feel free, like Kenyatta did?
15.   Learn what slave songs were about and why and how the songs were used in the enslaved quest for freedom. **Go to http://www.harriet-tubman.org/songs-of-the-underground-railroad**

> Learn about famous and lesser-known Africans and African Americans and have students do reports and interesting facts from individuals listed in quiz/activities #1, titled *Notable African and African American Figures in History*. Students can create flashcards by pasting pictures of the notable individuals on the front of the card and their bios on the back of the card and quiz one another. **Resources: List of African Americans (provides a list of African Americans by profession), wikipedia.org; List of African-American Firsts, wikipedia.org; 100 Greatest African Americans, wikipedia.org; African American Biographies, ducksters.com (Also use the wikipedia.org search engine to look up individuals by specific profession).*Kidsbritannica.com has short videos about some of the individuals that are noted and can be shown in class.**

> Do a project that allows students to find out what the enslaved built in America, as well as the work of notable African American Architects, like Paul Williams and the Egyptians who built the Pyramids.

Students can draw or create replicas of some of the buildings that enslaved people constructed or helped to construct. **See *African American Workers Built America,* clasp.org; businessinsider.com; whitehousehistory.org**

➤ Talk about or recreate inventions of notable African and/or African Americans. Students can make a traffic light with construction paper, to commemorate Garrett Morgan or make hearts to commemorate Dr. Daniel William Hale who performed the first open heart surgery. The list goes on of African American contributions. **Resources: *Black Inventors through American History, blackinventor.com; 120 things you probably didn't know were created by Black inventors, dailyhive.com; A-Z list of Black and African American Inventors,* interestingengineering.com**

➤ Learn by profession: Students can learn about African and/or African American aviators, individuals in the military, artists, educators, writers, inventors, doctors, cowboys, politicians, scientists, astronauts, athletes, architects, musicians, dancers of all forms of dance, advocates and more. Choose a career category and find out who of African/African American descent is/was in that field. For example: Astronauts: Ron McNair, Mae Jemison and students can list others or up to 3-5 individuals per category or whatever you choose. **Resources:** List of 100 African Americans; wikipedia.org (Also use wikipedia.org and place African American astronauts, cowboys, writers, or other specific occupations in search engine to find a list of names.

➤ Make a recipe book of what foods and recipes originated from Africa. Students can cut out or draw pictures of food items and specialties unique to Africa like, yams, plantains, rice, etc. and try to use some of the items at home to help prepare a meal like *jollof rice* which is a dish from West Africa. For the recipe go to thekitchen.com. (Also see "Six Foods Brought to The Americas To Help Keep African Culture Alive," at travelnoire.com/six-foods-America-African-culture-alive.

➤ Learn about Juneteenth and why it is celebrated in African American communities. **Resources:** (Book about Juneteenth – *Opal Lee: And What it Means to Be Free* by A. Duncan (Ages 4-8) Kids Connect offers down loadable worksheets on Juneteenth and other subjects for a nominal fee. More books are available as well as information including *17 Ways to Celebrate Juneteenth with Kids,* weareteachers.com

➤ Create African instruments like the Djembe drum and discover why they were important to African culture. See "Musical Instrument Crafts for Kids—Artists Helping Children" at https://www.artistshelpingchildren.org. This site includes information about making African drums.

➤ Listen to narratives of the enslaved, (as a class), on video or read some to your students of the ones the stories that are most age appropriate and have them write or express how they feel about the true stories.

➤ Find well done age-appropriate documentaries or videos to share with students/children and discuss (See *Resource* section for a list of videos)

➤ Start a monthly book club on age-appropriate books for your students on African and African American History. (See list of books in *Resource* section)

➤ Teach students about the significance of quilts in African American culture, which were often used to lead the enslaved to freedom when hung in certain positions in windows along the path of the Underground Railroad. Some squares of the quilt revealed clues to finding a way up North to freedom. Create a class or individual freedom quilt made of construction paper squares and allow students to create pieces of the quilt with words about freedom or symbols used by the enslaved and learn the meaning behind the symbol. (Book: *The Patchwork Path: A Quilt Map to Freedom* by B. Stroud. Ages 5-8)

➤ Learn about Kwanzaa, kids.nationalgeographic.com and How to Teach Kids about Kwanzaa, kidskonnect.com

➤ "What does family and/or friends mean to me?" Students can use copies of favorite family photos (with parent's permission) or draw pictures of family and/or friends, or bring in favorite mementos, etc. to display on a table that has been decorated with Kente cloth (students can use a long piece of butcher paper and color or paint it in a Kente pattern. Before placing the item on the table, students should be free to "show and tell" why their item(s) are important to them. Remind students how important family was to Kenyatta and enslaved children who were, in many cases, taken away from their families.

RESOURCES and TEACHER PREP TOOLS

Materials for <u>teachers</u> to review for preparation: These pages are for you! The following are resources and materials that are for optional use and may help in lesson enhancement and planning and gaining more knowledge about the subject of enslavement and African and African History. Due to the graphic nature and violence of enslavement and other forms of abuse after slavery, please review any materials listed below, beforehand to see what is appropriate to share with your students. Utilize your local and school library for listed books.

Brief Introduction: Articles, Videos and Overviews to Get Started

✓ *Elementary Students Talk about Slavery and Race Relations,* Voice of America News
✓ *The History of Slavery in America* (Part 1-3) YouTube.com
✓ MiAcademy Learning Channel – *An Introduction to Slavery in the United States*, YouTube
✓ "Teaching Hard History, American Slavery," learningforjustice.org
✓ *History of African Americans/Past to Future,* YouTube
✓ 10 'Must-Watch' Black History Documentaries, pbs.org
✓ USA Today article—"Slavery, Black History: Books, Movies, Lesson Plans for Kids, Adults"
✓ Overview of Slavery and Explanation, Answer Key section.

QUICK REFERENCE OF SUBJECT AREAS BY CATEGORY

ABOLITION MOVEMENT/UNDERGROUND RAILROAD

✓ "Abolitionist Movement," kids.britannica.com
✓ "The Superpower of Singing: Music and the Struggles Against Slavery,"nps.gov
✓ *Harriet Tubman's Escape to Freedom—video*
✓ *Dawn to Day: Stories from the Underground Railroad—video*

Joslyn Gaines Vanderpool

AFRICAN AMERICAN HISTORY

- ✓ *The African Americans*: *Many Rivers to Cross*, Henry Louis Gates, pbs.org—*video*
- ✓ "African Americans," kids.britannica.com
- ✓ "African American History Timeline," kids.britannica.com
- ✓ "Black Culture Connection, Classroom Resources for Educators,"pbs.org
- ✓ "Biographies of African Americans," ducksters.com
- ✓ *History of African Americans/Past to Future*, YouTube—video
- ✓ "Timeline of African American History in the United States," M. Hendricks, socialstudies.com
- ✓ "10 'Must-Watch' Black History Documentaries," pbs.org

AFRICAN ENSLAVEMENT IN AMERICA

- ✓ "Colonial America Slavery," ducksters.com
- ✓ Constitutional Rights Foundation – "Slavery in the American South," crf-usa.org
- ✓ *The History of Slavery in America (Part 1-3)*, youtube.com video
- ✓ "New England Colonies' Use of Slavery and Origins of Slavery," nationalgeographic.org
- ✓ *"Slavery in the United States,"* britannica.com
- ✓ "Life for Enslaved Men and Women," khanacademy.org
- ✓ "Treatment of Slaves," wikipedia.org

CIVIL RIGHTS ERA

- ✓ "Civil Rights Movement," history.com
- ✓ Civil Rights Facts for Kids, kids.britannica.com
- ✓ "Timeline of Civil Rights," ducksters.com
- ✓ *Civil Rights Era, Kids Academy video*
- ✓ *Eyes on the Prize Civil Rights Years 1954-1965*, Documentary (Ages 14+)
- ✓ *Martin Luther King Jr. for Kids,* YouTube—video

DECLARATION OF INDEPENDENCE/FOUNDING FATHERS

- ✓ "Declaration of Independence and Slavery," americanhistoryforkids.com, ushistory.org
- ✓ *How Many US Presidents Owned Slaves?"* history.com
- ✓ Maps of the World – *Which of the 13 Colonies Allowed Slavery?*
- ✓ *U.S. Constitutional Amendments*, constitutionfindlaw.com

LIFE AFTER SLAVERY

- ✓ "Black Codes and Jim Crow Laws," nationalgeographic.org; ducksters.com
- ✓ *Slavery by Another Name,* pbs.org—video
- ✓ "Reconstruction Era," ducksters.com; kids.britannica.com
- ✓ *Reconstruction: The Vote/Black History in Two Minutes,* Henry Louis Gates Jr.—video

RACE, SKIN COLOR, INCLUSION

- ✓ *Elementary Students talk about Slavery and Race Relations,* Voice of America News
- ✓ *Civil Rights Era, Kids Academy—video*
- ✓ *Little Rock Nine,* YouTube—video (Marquette University)

✓ *Sesame Street—We're Different, We're the Same and We're* All Wonderful (young readers)
✓ *Our Skin—First Conversation about Race* by Isabel Roxas (Ages 2-5)
✓ *PBS Kids Talk about Race and Racism*, pbs.org—*video*
✓ "Raising Race-Conscious Children: How to Talk to Kids about Race and Racism," by Beata Mostafavi, og.uofmhealth.org
✓ "Talking to Kids About Race and Racism," kidshealth.org

Videos on Black History (Tailored for Kids) Please Review First:

- *America's Journey Through Slavery: The Life of an Enslaved Person in America,* YouTube
- *Civil Rights Era, Kids Academy*
- *Dawn to Day: Stories from the Underground Railroad—video*
- *Harlem Renaissance Brainpop*, YouTube
- *Harriet Tubman's Escape to Freedom*, YouTube
- *Life of a Plantation Slave*, YouTube
- *MiAcademy Learning Channel – An Introduction to Slavery in the United States*, YouTube
- *Elementary Students talk about Slavery and Race Relations,* Voice of America News
- *15 Untold Black History Inventors Wasn't Taught At School*

MOVIES: *Hidden Figures*; (14+); Disney's *Ruby Bridges (Ages 9-12)*; 14 Movies About Race and Racism for Kids, womensday.com.

Websites— Must add subject or topic in the search engine, such as, "Abolitionist or Juneteenth."

- Americanhistoryforkids.com
- Blackhistory.com
- Blackpast.org
- Biography.com (Black History)
- Ducksters.com
- Historyforkids.org
- Kids.britannica.com (site has short video biographies)
- Kidsconnect.com
- Kidskiddle.com
- Library of Congress, loc.gov
- National Park Service, nps.gov
- National Museum of African American History and Culture, nmaahc.si.edu
- National Geographic Kids, nationalgeographic.com

Books about Enslavement for Young Readers. Check to see if these titles are in the school library. (This is not an exhaustive list):

(1) *Freedom Over Me: Eleven Slaves, Their Lives and Dreams Brought to Life* by A. Bryan (Ages 6-10)

(2) *The Kidnapped Prince: The Life of Olaudah Equiano* by O. Equiano, adapted by A. Cameron (Grades 3-7)

(3) *Opal Lee: And What it Means to Be Free* by A. Duncan (Ages 4-8)

(4) *Many Thousands Gone* by V. Hamilton (Ages 3-7)

(5) *Never Caught, the Story of Ona Judge* by E. Dunbar (Ages 9+)

(6) *Born on the Water* by N. Hannah-Jones (Ages 6-12)

(7) *Henry's Freedom Box* by E. Levine (Ages 4-8)

(8) *Moses: When Harriett Tubman Led her People to Freedom* by C. Boston Weatherford (Ages 4+)

(9) *Heart and Soul: The Story of Africans and African Americans* by K. Nelson (Ages 8-11)

(10) *If You Lived When There was Slavery in America* by A. Kamma (Grades 2-5)

(11)*The Patchwork Path: A Quilt Map to Freedom* by B. Stroud (Ages 5-8)

(12) *Before She was Harriet* by Cline-Ransome (Ages 4-8)

(13) *From Slave Ship to Freedom Road* by J. Lester (ages 8-12)

(14) *Frederick Douglass: The Last Days of Slavery* by W. Miller (Ages 5-8)

(15) *Show Way* by J. Woodson (Ages 4-8)

Young Readers Books About African and African American History. Check school or your local library to see if any of these titles or others are available (Not an exhaustive list):

(1) *ABC's of Black History* by R. Cortez (Ages 6-8)

(2) *Africa's Little Kings and Queens* by Kunda Kids (Ages 3-8)

(3) The Kulture Kidz -- *Learning About People Who Made a Difference* (Ages 6-12)

(4) *20th Century African American History for Kids: The Major Events that Shaped the Past and Present* History by M. Weston (Ages 8-12)

(5) *Black Heroes: A Black History Book for Kids: 51 Inspiring People from Ancient Africa to Modern Day USA* (People and Events in History) by A. Norwood (Ages 8-12)

(6) *The Story of Series Black History, Biography Books for New Readers* (Ages 6-9)

(7) *Mae Among the Stars*, by R. Ahmed (Ages 2-5)

(8) *Little Leaders: Bold Women in Black History* by V. Harrison (Ages 4-9)

(9) *Little Legends: Exceptional Men in Black History* by V. Harrison (Ages 8-12)

(10) *Have you Thanked an Inventor Today?* by P. Laurin (Ages 5-12)

(11) *Black Heroes: A Black History Book for Kids* by A. Norwood (Ages 8-12)

(12) *A Computer Called Katherine* by S. Slade (Ages 4-8)

(13) *Ruby Bridges Goes to School: My True Story* by R. Bridges (Ages 6-9)

Books about Sameness, Difference, Skin Color, Racial Tolerance

(1) Sesame Street—We're Different, We're the Same and We're All Wonderful (young readers)
(2) Our Skin—First Conversation about Race by Isabel Roxas (Ages 2-5)

Consider adding virtual or actual visits to museums or other places of historical relevance as field trips. Seek out virtual tours of African and African American museums or historical places. Check out "12 Black History Museums to Visit from Home," _; "12 of the Best Black History Museums in the US and Where to Find Them," tiqets.com; Other museums that may or may not offer virtual tours include the National Museum of African American History, the Whitney Plantation Museum, the National Underground Museum, the National Civil Rights Museum, the International African American Museum, the Legacy Museum.

STUDENT CORNER

STUDENT HAND-OUTS

List of Websites Hand-out

Bonus Quiz—What do you know about African and African American Innovators?

- Quiz #1 Notable African/African Figures in History
-
- Quiz #2 Who Said or Did It? (Chapters 1-4)
-
- Quiz #3 African Words
-
- Quiz #4 English to African Paragraph Rewrite
-
- Quiz #5 Name Where It Happened: African or America
-
- Quiz #6 Multiple Choice
-
- Quiz #7 True/False
-
- Quiz #8 Word Scramble (Older Students)
-
- Quiz #9 Word List (Younger Students)
-
- Quiz #10 Random Word List Activity (Younger Students)
-
- Quiz #11 Word Study List (Older Students)
-
- Quiz #12 Word Scramble 1-4 (Younger Students)

VILLAGE CIRCLES – DISCUSSION

- Free Thought Discussions/ Kenyatta Assignment

- Terms to Know Activity (Older Students)

- Overview: Enslavement in America and Life After the Civil War – What Do You Know?

WHAT DO YOU KNOW ABOUT AFRICAN AMERICAN INNOVATORS? Place a check by items that you believe were created by African American innovators and then research the names below to see who created what.

Potato Chips

Golf Tee

Hairbrush

Traffic Light

Doorknob

First Clock in the U.S.

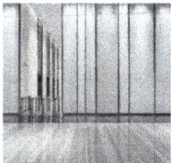

Elevator doors

Refrigerated Trucks

1st Heart Surgery

Ice Cream Scooper

Fire Escape Ladder

Secured U.S. Postal Boxes

Shoe Making Machine

Benjamin Banneker; Alfred L. Cralle; George Crum; Osbourn Dorsey; Philip Downing; Dr. George Grant; Frederick McKinley Jones; Jan Matzeliger; Alexander Miles; Garrett Morgan; Lyda D. Newman; Joseph Richard Winters; Dr. Daniel Hale Williams. Sources: study.com; the Black Inventors Museum; oprahdaily.com; history.com; "List of African American inventors and scientists," wikipedia.org

LIST OF WEBSITES HAND-OUT (For Older Students and Teachers)

This handout provides various websites where you might find information and answers to, and about, some of the questions in Quiz #1, and the Project, Free Thought Discussions, Terms to Know and the Overview of Enslavement sections, which are listed in parentheses. For the answers to Quizzes 2-10, read and study *Kenyatta's Stone*.

☀ Tip: A parentheses looks like this with words inside ( ).

Where You Might Find the Answers to the Information in Parentheses

A
1. "African Americans at a Glance" — **kids.britannica.com.** (*Quiz #1* and *Project* section)
2. "African Americans: List of African Americans"— **wikipedia.org.** (*Quiz #1* and *Project* section)
3. "African American Children (Enslaved)" — **nps.gov**; (*Free Thought* and *Overview* sections*)
4. "African American Civil Rights Movement"— **ducksters.com; kids.britannica.com** (*Quiz #1, Terms to Know, Free Thought, Overview* sections)
5. "Abolitionist Movement" — **kids-britannica.com; m.american-historama.org.** (*Quiz #1, Terms to Know, Overview* sections*)
6. "African Flags" — **ducksters.com.** (*Project* section)
7. "The American Civil War" — **historyforkids.org; ducksters.com.** (*Free Thought, Overview* sections).
8. "American Civil War Reconstruction" — **historyforkids.org; ducksters.com** (*Terms to Know, Overview* sections)
9. "American Amendments" — **historyforkids.org** (*Free Thought, Terms to Know, Overview* sections)
10. "Ancient Egypt Inventions and Technology" — **ducksters.com; historyforkids.org** (*Project* section)
11. "Ancient Africa" — **ducksters.com** (*Project* section)
12. "A-Z list of Black and African American inventors" — **interestingengineering.com** (*Project* section)

B
1. "Black/African American Inventors" — **blackinventors.com; biography.com** (*Project* section)
2. "Black Inventors: *120 things you probably didn't know were created by Black inventors*" – **dailyhive.com** (*Project* section)
3. "Black Codes and Jim Crow Laws"— **nationalgeographic.org; ducksters.com** (*Terms to Know, Overview* sections)

C-J
1. "Civil Rights the History of Slavery in the United States" — **ducksters.com** (*Terms to Know, Free Thought, Overview* sections)
2. "Colonial America, Slavery" — **ducksters.com** (*Terms to Know, Free Thought, Overview* sections)
3. "Civil Rights Act of 1964 Facts for Kids" — **historyforkids.org** (*Overview, Terms to Know* sections)
4. "Declaration of Independence" — **ducksters.com** (*Terms to Know, Free Thought, Overview, Project* sections)
5. "Dred Scott Decision" — **wikipedia.org; historyforkids.org** (*Quiz #1*)
6. "Emancipation Proclamation"— **historyforkids.org** (*Free Thought, Terms to Know, Overview* sections)

7. "Free States" — **worldpopulationreview.com** (*Project, Free Thought, Overview* sections)
8. *"Fugitive Slave Laws" —***kids.britannica.com** *(Terms to Know, Overview, Free Thought sections)*
9. "Juneteenth Facts and Information" — **wikipedia.org** (*Terms to Know, Project, Overview* sections)

L-Z

1. "List of Presidents who Owned Slaves" — **wikipedia.org** (*Overview* section)
2. *"Reconstruction African Americans" —* **historyforkids.org, bbc.co.uk** *(Terms to Know, Overview sections)*
3. "Slave States" — **worldpopulationreview.com; wikipedia.org** (*Project, Overview* sections)
4. "Singing in Slavery: Songs of Survival, Songs of Freedom" — **_;** (*Project, Terms to Know* sections)
5. "Treatment of the Enslaved" — **ducksters.com** (*Terms to Know, Free Thought* sections)
6. *Underground Railroad,* **video** — **kids.britannica.com; ducksters.com** (*Terms to Know, Projects* sections)
7. "The Union States" — **historyforkids.org** (*Terms to Know, Overview, Free Thought* sections)
8. "United States Declaration of Independence" — **historyforkids.org** (*Projects, Free Thought, Overview* sections)
9. "Voting Rights Act of 1965" — **historyforkids.org; kids.britannica.com; kidskiddle.com** (*Overview* section)
10. "What are the 13th, 14th and 15th Amendments" — **ducksters.com; kids.britannica.com; wikipedia.org** (*Free Thought, Terms to Know, Overview* sections)
11. "What Kind of Jobs Did Enslaved African Americans Do?" — **jyfmuseums.org** (*Free Thought, Overview* sections)
12. "What Kind of Challenges Did Free People Face?"— **historyforkids.org** (*Terms to Know, Free Thought, Overview* sections)

Quiz/Activity #1

LOOK IT UP – NOTABLE AFRICAN AND AFRICAN AMERICANS IN HISTORY (Handout). Find out which of the notable figures listed below, were enslaved? How many were children who might have possibly been enslaved based on their age and where he/she was born?

☼   TIP: Look Up each name below to find out who is who. Resource: wikiepedia.org; kids.brittanca.org

(A) Frederick Douglas (B) Martin Luther King, Jr. (C) Sojourner Truth (D) Phillis Wheatly (E) Dred Scott (F) Harriet Tubman (G) Marian Anderson (H) Crispus Attucks (I) Benjamin Banneker (J) Fannie Lou Hamer (K) Jackie Robinson (L) Mae Jemison (M) Cudjoe Lewis (N) Cathay Williams (O) Gwendolyn Brooks (P) Bessie Coleman (Q) Henry Ossian Flipper (R) Stagecoach Mary Fields (S) Garrett Morgan (T) Barak Obama (U) Nat Turner (V) Ida B. Wells (W) Dr. Daniel Hale Williams (X) Langston Hughes (Y) Sidney Poitier (Z) Amos Fortune

1. This person was the first African American woman and Native American licensed pilot. _____

2. This person was a soldier, and the first African American to graduate from West Point U.S. Military Academy. _____

3. This person led more than 300 enslaved to freedom and was called the Moses of her people. _____

4. This person invented gas mask, traffic signal and other items. _____

5. This person was the first African American woman star route carrier of the United States mail. She rode the Pony Express. _____

6. First African American author of a published book of poetry in the United States. _____

7. Performed the first heart surgery and established first Black-run hospital. _____

8. Opera singer who performed on the steps of the Lincoln Memorial in Washington, DC in 1939. _____

9. He was the first African American to break the National Baseball League color line. _____

10. She pretended to be a man to join the United States Army. _____

11. He was the first African American president of the United States. _____

12. He led a major revolt against slavery. _____

13. He was the first African American actor to win a *Best Actor* Oscar in 1964. _____

14. This person was the first Black woman in space and an astronaut. She's also a doctor and engineer. _____

15. This person was the third to last Africans brought to America, as a slave, on the Clotilda. _____

16. This person was a farmer who wrote almanacs and invented one of the first clocks in America. _____

17. This person became an abolitionist who asked, "Ain't I a Woman Too?" _____

18. This person was a brilliant orator, who fought to abolish slavery and is one of the most important African Americans in history. _____

19. This person was a young prince in Africa and enslaved in America. He bought his freedom at age 60. _____

20. This person was a sailor and a whaler who was the first man killed in the American Revolution. _____

21. This person was a writer, poet and leader of the Harlem Renaissance. _____

22. This person picked 200-300 pounds of cotton daily at age 13 when she had polio; and was a civil rights activist from Mississippi who said, "I'm sick and tired of being sick and tired." _____

23. This person was the most famous civil rights movement activist and leader in the world. He had "A Dream" _____

24. This person is the first African American to win a Pulitzer Prize for poetry in 1950. _____

25. This journalist and civil and women's rights activist helped found the *(NAACP) _____

26. This person went to the Supreme Court to ask for his freedom, but he lost his case. _____

*National Association for the Advancement of Colored People

Quiz/Activity #2 (Chapters 1-4)

WHO SAID OR DID IT? *FROM KENYATTA'S STONE CHAPTER 1*
(Handout) Follow your teacher's instructions.

Questions from Chapter 1:

1. Who said, "No it's too much cloth. No cloth today!" _____

2. Who washed their hair in the cool misty sea, and tended to their father's peanut

soup? _____

3.Who talked about traveling across the river to Benta Town and meeting a young flute

maker? _____

4. Who made chocolate paste under the cacao tree? _____and _____

5. Who helped Umama make dinner? _____and _____

6. Who took Kenyatta to the woods and taught her how to use leaves to make trails and

mark the trees? _____

7. Who made Nana furious? _____

WHO SAID OR DID IT? *FROM KENYATTA'S STONE CHAPTER 2*
(Handout) Follow your teacher's instructions.

1. Who asked, "Why do they chain up people whose skin is like ours? What have we done?"

_____

2. Who said, "Do you have a dog in your throat?" _____

3. Who cried nearly all day, every day on the slave ship? _____ and

_____

4. Who wished their legs weren't wobbly so that they could "run to freedom, run to family, run

to the misty cool sea?" _____

5. Who said, "We are going to be sold as slaves in America. We will have to work in the fields

for the rest of our lives! They will beat us when they want to, and we will never see Africa

again?" _____

6. Who hid Kozo from the slave traders? _____

WHO SAID OR DID IT? *FROM KENYATTA'S STONE CHAPTER 3*
(Handout) Follow your teacher's instructions.

1. Who did not get to attend school? _____ and _____

2. Who said to Kenyatta, "I will be with you in spirit?" _____

3. Who said, "Girl, we are going to sell you for running?" _____

4. Who told Kenyatta to "Keep Africa in your heart and teach the others about our beautiful country and the meaning of freedom?" _____

5. Who chanted, "Africa! Africa! We want Africa?" _____

6. Who got lost after several hours of stumbling in the dark? _____ and

_____

WHO SAID OR DID IT? *FROM KENYATTA'S STONE CHAPTER 4*
(Handout) Follow your teacher's instructions.

1. Who won the captain's trust? _____

2. Who bit the captain's finger? _____

3. Who hid Kozo in a pot? _____

4. Who helped Kenyatta find her family after Nana Tala was too tired to travel? _____

5. Who jumped out of the bed and danced upon seeing Kenyatta and Kozo? _____

6. Who thanked Nana Tala by saying, "Thank you Nana Tala for watching over our Kenyatta and Kozo.

We are grateful to you sir"? _____

Quiz/Activity #3

AFRICAN WORDS: Match the English Word with the Meaning in the (*Twi) African Language by putting the letters for the African terms next to the correct English version of the word. (If you're not sure, ask your teacher if you can look at page 3 and 16 of your Kenyatta's Stone book to find the answers.

1. Grandfather_____   A. Umama

2. Mother_____   B. Utata

3. Sister_____   C. Oyere

4. Grandson_____   D. Onuabarima

5. Grandmother_____   E. Abofra

6. Brother_____   F. Nana (Can use 2 times)

7. Wife_____   G. Onuabaa

8. Father_____

Extra Credit:

If you have an umama, write down the first name of your umama _____

If you have a utata write down the first name of your utata _____

If you have a nana, (hint it could be more than one person) write down the first name(s) of your

Nana _____ Nana _____

If you have a Onuabaa, write down their name or names

_____

If you have a Onuabarima, write down their name or names

_____

Are you an Abofra? _____

*Twi Language: Spoken by the Akan people in Southern and Central Ghana. **Source: wikipedia.org**

QUIZ/ACTIVITY #4

ENGLISH TO TWI AFRICAN PARAGRAPH REWRITE

Please read the paragraph below. The words for **GRANDMOTHER, GRANDFATHER, GRANDSON, MOTHER, FATHER, SISTER, BROTHER, AND WIFE ARE IN ENGLISH.** After reading the paragraph, go down to **paragraph #2** and change the words that are in bold letters and underlined into the correct Twi African words and place in the spaces provided to recreate the paragraph again but with the correct Twi African words.

Review pages 3 and 16 in the *Kenyatta's Stone* book for help. Here are the words you will be using: **UTATA, UMAMA, NANA, OYERE, ABOFRA, ONUABARIMA, ONUABAA. HINT: ONE OF THE WORDS IS USED TWO TIMES.**

PARAGRAPH #1

My **Grandmother**, Lily, and **Grandfather**, Henry, live in Utah. I am their **grandson**, Shay. I live in Iowa with my **mother** and **father** and with my **sister**, Tara, and my **brother**, Jordan. My Uncle James and his **wife** live next door.

PARAGRAPH #2 – Now it's your turn to use the correct African words.

My (**Grandmother**, Lily) USE THE TWI AFRICAN WORD FOR GRANDMOTHER

HERE _____ and (**Grandfather**, Henry) *USE THE TWI AFRICAN WORD FOR*

GRANDFATHER HERE _____ live in Utah. I am their (**grandson**, Shay) *USE THE*

TWI WORD FOR GRANDSON HERE _____ . I live in Iowa with my (**mother**) *USE*

THE TWI AFRICAN WORD FOR MOTHER HERE _____ and (**father**) *USE THE*

TWI AFRICAN WORD FOR FATHER HERE _____ and with my (**sister**), Tara.

USE THE TWI AFRICAN WORD FOR SISTER HERE _____ and my (**brother**,

Jordan) *USE THE TWI AFRICAN WORD FOR BROTHER HERE* _____ . My

Uncle James lives next door with his (**wife**). *USE THE TWI AFRICAN WORD FOR WIFE*

HERE _____ .

Quiz/Activity #5

NAME WHERE IT HAPPENED: AFRICA OR AMERICA? (Hand-Out) Please name where the following events happened. Or follow your teacher's instructions.

1. Kenyatta was sold on an auction block _____

2. Nana bought Kenyatta mangoes _____

3. Kenyatta's mother danced at festivals _____

4. Kenyatta and Nana Tala were separated _____

5. Kenyatta was free to roam _____

6. Kenyatta worked in the fields _____

7. Kenyatta and her friend played under the cacao tree _____

8. Kenyatta heard singing coming from the ship _____

9. Umama Sallie told Kenyatta to believe! _____

10. Kozo made the other children laugh _____

11. Nana Tala hid Kozo under his wraps _____

12. The villagers gathered around when Kenyatta's father played his flute

    _____

13. Kenyatta tried to escape but got lost _____

14. The food was delicious and plentiful _____

15. The clothes were bright and colorful _____

16. Kenyatta fell asleep to stories about far off places with bands of animals

    _____

17. Kenyatta placed her stone on Nana Tala's heart _____

18. The houses did not look like huts _____

19. Where Kenyatta was happiest _____

20. Kenyatta taught the others to make necklaces from berries and make flutes _____

Quiz/Activity #6

MULTIPLE CHOICE QUESTIONS

Please circle the correct letter A or B

1. Kenyatta and the enslaved children worked

   A. Only on Sundays   B. Every day except Sundays

2. Kenyatta loved wearing

   A. Gray, drab clothes   B. Colorful clothes

3. Kenyatta's father spoke about the power of

   A. The bees and birds   B. The sea and trees

4. Kenyatta dreamt about...

   A. Elephants, zebras, gazelles   B. Dolphins, Whales, and Fish

5. Where did Kenyatta live in Africa?

   A. House   B. Hut

6. Where did Kenyatta live in America?

   A. Inside the Ames house   B. In a shed

7. Kenyatta's best friend was

   A. Madelyn   B. Matawan

8. Kenyatta and her friend liked

   A. Playing in the sea   B. Sitting beneath the cacao tree

9. Kenyatta's mother looked like an

   A. African Queen   B. Dancing Queen

10. The African word that Kenyatta called her father was

   A. Umama   B. Utata

11. Nana Tala was Kenyatta and Kozo's

   A. Adopted Grandfather   B. Uncle

12. Kenyatta broke the stone because

   A. She was upset and wanted to get back to Africa and wanted the other enslaved children to feel the magic of Africa.

   B. She was happy with her life in America and wanted to get rid of the stone.

Quiz/Activity #7

✓ **TRUE/ FALSE QUESTIONNAIRE:** (Hand-out) Use extra paper if needed. Follow your teacher's instructions.

1. Kenyatta loved her life in Africa _____ If Kenyatta loved her life in Africa, list 3 things she did and loved about Africa.

2. Kenyatta's Nana, (Grandmother) loved when Kozo ate the berries _____ If grandmother Nana loved Kozo, how did she show it?

3. When the slave traders came to Kenyatta's hut, she was tending to her father's carrot soup_____ If it was not carrot soup, what type of soup was it?

4. When Kenyatta was taken from her home in Africa, she was not afraid _____ If this is or is not true, what did she do if she was taken?

5. The slave traders who took Kenyatta politely asked her if she wanted to go with them _____ If they were not polite, how did they treat Kenyatta?

6. The slave ship was clean with plenty of room for everyone to move about _____ If the ship was not this way, how was it?

7. The enslaved children were laughing on the ship _____ If they were not laughing, what were they doing? How did they feel?

8. Kenyatta and the other enslaved children did not miss their families _____ If they did miss their families, how did they feel? What emotions did they have?

9. Kenyatta had a lot of food to eat on the ship and enjoyed it _____ If this is true or not true, please say what Kenyatta ate on the ship? How often did she eat on the ship?

10. Kenyatta met an older gentleman on the ship who was kind to her _____ If she did meet someone on the ship, who was that person and what did that person do for Kenyatta?

11. Kenyatta was sold on an auction block in America _____ If Kenyatta was sold, what was done to her?

12. Kenyatta did not have to work in the fields in America; she played all day _____ If she did have to work, what type of work did she do?

13. Kenyatta and the other enslaved children got to go to school _____ If this is not true, why didn't they go to school? What did they have to do?

14. Kenyatta wanted to leave America _____ If Kenyatta wanted to leave America, why did she want to leave?

15. Kenyatta wanted the other enslaved children to know about Africa _____ If Kenyatta wanted the other enslaved children and Billy and Mary Ames to know about Africa, why was it important for her to teach them?

16. Kenyatta taught the other children how to make drums _____. If this is false, what did she teach them to make? List everything you can remember from the story that Kenyatta taught the others.

17. Umama Sallie did not run away from the Ames Plantation _____ If this is true, why did or didn't Umama Sallie try to leave and return to Africa?

18. When Kenyatta got tired of slavery she could just walk away and leave anytime she wanted to _____ If this is or is not true explain why?

19. Kenyatta ran away from the Ames Plantation with Kozo and never got caught_____ If this is true, or untrue what happened when she tried to escape?

20. Kenyatta placed the stone on her heart _____ If she did, why do you think she placed it on her heart?

QUIZ/ACTIVITY #8

WORD SCRAMBLE Your teacher will assign and give each team hand-outs face down (no peeking). When the teacher says, "GO!" Flip over your paper and work with team to unscramble the letters to form the ten words below as fast as you can. Speak quietly in your group and don't let another team hear your answers. When you hear "TIMES UP!" stop. If your team finishes before the teacher says, "TIMES UP!" raise your hands and say you're done. Be prepared to talk about how the words and how they relate to Kenyatta's story. See Example of word unscrambled: **TENTAYAK = KENYATTA.**

1. CANDIUTOE

2. MODFEER

3. UACIONT LOBCK

4. HIPS

5. EPACRUT

6. AVGOYE

7. HANICS

8. YAMFIL

9. CAPESE

10. VABRE

WORD LIST FOR YOUNGER STUDENTS

Test #1

1. Soup
2. Sea
3. Tail
4. Free
5. Cry

Test #2

1. Wag
2. Hut
3. Cloth
4. Happy
5. Mat

Test #3

1. School
2. Stone
3. Hot
4. Run
5. Dog

Test #4

1. Ship
2. Tree
3. Pot
4. Sleep
5. Lap

QUIZ #10 Younger Students Random Word List Quiz/Activity—Put the correct word under each picture from your Spelling List.

_____

_____

_____

_____

_____

_____

_____

_____

_____

_____

Quiz/Activity #11

WORD STUDY LIST FOR OLDER STUDENTS (Look up each word's meaning and be prepared to spell each word(s) and use words with a star in a sentence.)

*Abolish	Equality	Quakers
African Descent	Escape	*Resilient
American Revolution	Family	Restrict
Auction Block	Forcibly	*Revolt
Border States	*Freedom	Secede
Brave	Free State	Segregation
*Capture	*Humanity	Seized
Citizenship	Importation	Servitude
Confederacy States	Indentured Servant	Sharecropper
Continental Congress	Integration	Slave State
Discrimination	Little Rock Nine	States' Rights
Economy	*Livelihood	Union States
*Elusive	Missouri Compromise	*Voyage
Emancipation	*Prohibit	
Enslavement	Provisions	

Quiz/Activity # 12 (Younger Students)

WORD SCRAMBLE #1

POUS

Kenyatta's father loved peanut _____.

EAS

Kenyatta lived by the misty cool blue _____.

LAIT

Kozo liked to wag his _____.

EFRE

Kenyatta wanted to be _____.

RYC

When the enslaved children were taken from their families, they would _____ all day.

WORD SCRAMBLE #2

CLOOSH

Kenyatta and the other enslaved children could not go to _____.

TONES

Nana Tala gave Kenyatta a magical _____.

TOH

In Africa and America the weather is sometimes _____.

NUR

Kenyatta was unhappy being a slave, so she wanted to _____away.

GDO

Kozo wasn't a cat, but he was a _____.

WORD SCRAMBLE #3

AWG

When Kozo was happy, he would _____ his tail.

THU

When Kenyatta was in Africa, she lived in a _____.

TAM

In America, Kenyatta slept on a _____.

UFLTE

Kenyatta's father played the _____.

PAPYH

In Africa, Kenyatta had a _____ life.

WORD SCRAMBLE #4

HISP

Kenyatta and other Africans were chained together on a big _____.

RETE

Matawan and Kenyatta played under the cacao _____.'

OPT

Nana Tala hid Kozo away from the captain in a _____.

PLEES

Kenyatta fell into a light _____ after crying for hours.

PAL

Umama Sallie pulled Kenyatta on her _____ to comfort her.

Free Thought Questions: Possible Topics to Discuss about Kenyatta's Stone
(Questions can be led by teachers)

Kenyatta said, "Slavery means no freedom to roam."

Kenyatta once knew freedom, family love, and happiness and longed to experience it again. She was given a chance to return to her homeland and have her dream fulfilled, which wasn't true for many enslaved people in America. Some lived their entire lives enslaved. In a group setting or village circle, feel free to discuss the following, a few topics at a time and allow students to ask questions too. You, as the teacher, can ask the questions of the students, a few at a time, or as many questions as you'd like per session:

WHAT RIGHTS DID THE ENSLAVED HAVE? Could the enslaved get married? Could they attend school? Could they go on vacations? Could they eat whenever they wanted and whatever they wanted? Did they have a choice about where they wanted to live? Could the enslaved have their own homes? Could the enslaved refuse to do the work their owners gave them? If not, then why?

THE DECLARATION OF INDEPENDENCE

According to the Declaration of Independence, which was an important document signed by the founding fathers of the United States, there are three basic ideas that are included that should have applied to all people of the United States:

> ➤ "All men are created equal, and have the rights of life, liberty and the pursuit of happiness."

> ➤ "The main business of the government is to protect these rights."

> ➤ "If the government tries to withhold these rights, the people are free to revolt and set up a new government."

Source: Britannica Encyclopedia

To enslave is to own another person, forcing them to work without pay, keeping them against their will and not giving them any basic rights or freedoms. What are the rights you have today?

Of life, liberty and the pursuit of happiness, which word means freedom?

What do you believe pursuit of happiness means?

What does being equal mean? Does it mean every person in America having the same rights? Or not?

Do you have freedom and the rights found in the Declaration of Independence, such as life, liberty and the pursuit of happiness?

What does freedom mean to you?

Do you think Kenyatta was happy, or felt equal when she was enslaved? Why or why not?

How were the enslaved Africans treated from the time they and Kenyatta were captured in Africa, to the voyage on the ship, to when their lives began in America?

From the book, what did the older gentleman on the ship who spoke to Nana Tala, say about slavery when he found out what was going to happen to the enslaved just before they got off the ship in America?

How did Kenyatta feel when she thought she would never see her family again? Think of each family member or person in Kenyatta's life, Umama, Utata, Nana, Nana Tala, Umama Sallie, Matawan, and Kozo and what they meant to her.

What do your family and friends mean to you?

How did Kenyatta and Tala feel when they were separated after arriving in America? Were they sad, angry, afraid?

How was Kenyatta's life different in Africa than in America? Give examples of what she did in Africa and what she did in America that were not the same.

Did Kenyatta feel free in Africa? What does freedom mean to you? What makes you feel free or not feel free?

In slave states, it was against the law for enslaved people to go to school to learn. Did Kenyatta and the other enslaved children get to go to school? What does going to school mean to you? Why do you think enslaved children were not allowed to go to school?

Teacher or student can read the following passage:

Frederick Douglass, who was born into slavery in about 1818, would become one of the greatest speakers in the world and a well-known abolitionist. He spoke passionately and eloquently against slavery and supported freedom and rights for African Americans and women.

As a youth, he was taught the alphabet by his Mistress, Mrs. Auld, but when Master Auld found out, he told his wife it was illegal to teach a slave to read and forbade anymore lessons. According to Frederick's narrative, Master Auld said, that "If a slave learned to read, it would forever unfit him from being a slave. He would at once become unmanageable, and no value to his master." Young Frederick was even more determined to read, so he found a way to learn because he knew that by doing so, he would find a way to be free. When he set off to do errands in town, he always took a book and befriended poor white children along the way who he asked to teach him to read in exchange for scraps of bread. Some helped him for free. **Source:** wikipedia.org; nps.gov; biography.com

What was it really like to be a child who was enslaved? Think about Kenyatta? What age did enslaved children have to begin working? What things do you think they had to do? Did they have toys, or did they have to make their own, like Kenyatta did? What did Kenyatta make or do to entertain herself and the other children?

Nana Tala told Kenyatta that she came from a strong people. How was Kenyatta strong, brave, and courageous?

Were the others that were enslaved also brave? What did they have to go through daily?

What did Kenyatta say and do to let you know that she was unhappy and upset with being enslaved? Discuss how and why Kenyatta wanted to escape? Who is Harriet Tubman, Fredrick Douglass? How was Kenyatta like they were?

Kenyatta asked Nana Tala, why they were taken away from Africa? Did she do anything wrong to become enslaved?

What do you think is wrong about enslaving other people?

Kenyatta Assignment

Could Kenyatta Have Really Returned Home?

Extra Questions Handout

This is a chance to team up and learn about the following and come back at a later date to discuss the topic as a group. Use extra paper if needed to answer the questions.

In your opinion, could Kenyatta have really returned to Africa? Give your reasons why or why not? Afterward, read about **Abdulrahman Ibrahim Ibn Sori**; wikipedia.org; theafrica.know.org; and **Amos Fortune**, amosfortune.com and wikipedia.org; and **Olaudah Equiano**, blackpast.org.

How are Abdulrahman Ibrahim Ibn Sori, Amos Fortune, and Prince Olaudah Equiano, like Kenyatta? Were they all from Africa?

Were Abdulrahman Ibrahim Ibn Sori, Amos Fortune and Prince Olaudah Equiano enslaved as children, like Kenyatta? Were any of them free before being enslaved? Did they become free again? If they did, how did they become free?

What happened to Abdulrahman Ibrahim Ibn Sori when he returned to Africa, also happened to Nana Tala when he returned to Africa. What happened to them?

What is the Republic of Liberia and what happened there between 1820-1864?

Bonus Question: Why Is it important to learn about each other's histories? Is American and World History about only one group of people or many groups of people from different/diverse cultures, and ethnic backgrounds who helped shape the world? If it is about different people who shaped the world, do a project about different/diverse groups of people and what contributions they made to shape the world.

Terms to Know: Work as a team or individually to find out about the words below. Share with the class, the meaning of the words, after all teams have reported. See what you know by taking a quiz together to determine what terms matches with the definitions provided on the right side of the following pages. Many answers for the following questions can be found using the *List of Websites* Handout, wikipedia.org; nationalgeographic.org; ducksters.com, kids.britannica.com; historyforkids.org; kidskiddle.com; YouTube: A Brief History: The Harlem Renaissance

1. Abolitionists
2. Black Codes/Jim Crow Laws
3. Civil Rights Movement
4. Civil War
5. Emancipation Proclamation
6. Supreme Court
7. Freedom Songs
8. Freedmen's Bureau
9. Forced Slave Labor
10. Fugitive Slave Laws
11. Harlem Renaissance
12. Juneteenth
13. Middle Passage
14. Reconstruction Period
15. Slave Revolt/Rebellion
16. Underground Railroad (Video YouTube: *Harriet Tubman's Escape to Freedom*)
17. 13th, 14th, and 15th Amendments

DID YOU LOOK UP THE TERMS? Now it is your turn to see what you know. Use the list provided of *Terms to Know* to answer the questions below by placing a number on the line provided.

1. _____ It is a yearly celebration to remember the enslaved that did not get word in the state of Texas that they were free until June 19, 1865, although, all enslaved had been freed by President Abraham Lincoln in January 1863.

2. _____ It was a document to free the enslaved signed by President Abraham Lincoln on January 3, 1863.

3. _____ They thought slavery was wrong and did not believe that one group of people should own another group of people.

4. _____ A time in the 1950s and 1960s when black people marched to gain their freedom and justice. Led by such notable people as Rosa Parks, Roy Wilkins, Ella Baker, Martin L. King Jr., and many others.

5. _____ During the 1920s Black artists, writers and poets had established an important presence in an area of New York City

6. _____ These were created to keep the enslaved from running away. The enslaved could be captured and returned to slavery, even if they escaped to a free state.

7. _____ This was not a train at all, but a system that ran through the North up to Canada to help runaway slaves escape from being enslaved. It was a series of houses, barns, places were the enslaved could hide from their owners, masters, and fugitive slave hunters, who sought to return them to slavery.

8. _____ This was the route across the Atlantic Ocean that the enslaved were brought in ships from Africa to the Americas. Many of the enslaved did not survive the journey.

9. _____ These were established for years after slavery to keep black people in certain places and states from having certain rights, which included, voting, sitting anywhere they wanted on public transportation or living where they wanted to live, etc.

10. _____ This decision-making group is the law of the land and makes many decisions regarding rights for the United States of America. Some of those decisions have been about the rights of African American people.

11. _____ These ideals and acts of Congress helped end slavery and gave black people some limited rights.

12. _____ The only war where Americans fought against Americans in the North and South portion of the United States. The goal of President Lincoln was to keep all the states together and not separate. Some believed it was about issues of slavery and helped bring slavery to an end.

13. _____ This organization set up schools for former slaves after the Civil War.

14. _____ During slavery many tried to escape and fought against being treated as less than human, with no rights or freedoms, so they fought back with the help of other slaves, and sometimes abolitionists. What is this called when the enslaved tried to end slavery or gain freedom.

15. _____ When someone is owned by another person and has no rights and no choice about their own life and has to work for free.

16. _____ Time period after slavery.

17. _____The enslaved wanted to escape slavery desperately and used these to express their sadness or desire to be free. These also were a way to communicate and give clues to other enslaved people about how to survive and try to escape.

Overview: Enslavement in America and After – What Do You Know? More Free Thought

Important Note: Enslavement has been around since the beginning of time and occurred in many places such as Africa, China, Europe, India, Pakistan, the Middle East, the West Indies and many other regions. For this assignment we are focusing on the institution of slavery in the United States (Use the List of Websites Handout and the Slavery Through the Civil Rights Movement Timeline for help with finding answers). Then discuss as a class.

1. What year did the enslavement of African/African Americans start in this country and when did it end?

2. Why was there Slavery in America?

3. Why were most of those enslaved in America of African descent?

4. How many Africans were brought to America and how many enslaved were in America in 1860?

5. Which of the 13 American colonies allowed slavery?

6. What is the Declaration of Independence and why didn't it apply to the enslaved?

7. Were there any U.S. presidents who owned slaves? If so name them.

8. What were some of the tasks and chores of the enslaved? Name at least 3

9. Were the enslaved separated from their families?

10. Why were the enslaved forbidden from going to school?

11. What type of foods were slaves given to eat?

12. Thinking back to Kenyatta's story, did the enslaved attempt to escape or protest about slavery and having freedom?

13. Were there revolts and rebellions against slavery. If so, name a few of the people who revolted or were abolitionists?

14. Why did some states do away with slavery?

15. When the Civil War started, how many states were slave states and how many were free? Please name those states that were free and which states were not.

16. Why did the Civil War start, and did it end slavery?

17. What are the Thirteenth, Fourteenth and Fifteenth Amendments?

18. What happened to the enslaved after slavery? Think of the Reconstruction Era.

19. What is the Civil Rights Act of 1964?

20. Why do you think that Dr. Martin Luther King, Jr., like Kenyatta had a dream about freedom?

21. How were African Americans treated in the United States from 1865, up to the Civil Rights Act of 1964 to today?

22. How do you think YOU can make the world a better place?

NOTES FOR EDUCATORS (ANSWER KEYS):

BONUS ASSIGNMENT: All items were created by innovators of African descent.

Matching Innovator with Product: Potato Chips, (George Crum); Golf Tee, (Dr. George Grant); Hair Brush, (Lyda D. Newman); Traffic Light, (Garrett Morgan); Door Knob, (Osbourn Dorsey); First Clock, (Benjamin Banneker); Elevator Doors, (Alexander Miles); Refrigerated Trucks, (Frederick McKinley Jones); First Successful Heart Surgery, (Dr. Daniel Hale Williams); Ice Cream Scooper, (Alfred L. Cralle); Fire Escape Ladder, (Joseph Richard Winters); Shoe Making Machine, (Jan Matzeliger); Secured US Postal Mailbox, (Philip Downing).

Q/A #1. AFRICAN AMERICAN NOTABLE FIGURES WHO WERE ENSLAVED: A, C, D, E, F, H, M, N, Q, R, U, V, Z. **Those enslaved as children or youth:** A, C, D, E, F, H, N, Q, R, U, V, Z

Q/A #1. Identities of African American Notables: (1) **P**—Bessie Coleman (2) **Q**—Henry Ossian Flipper (3) **F**— Harriet Tubman (4) **S**—Garrett Morgan (5) **R**—Stage Coach Mary Fields (6) **D**—Phillis Wheatly (7) **W**—Daniel Hale Williams (8) **G**—Marion Anderson (9) **K**—Jackie Robinson (10) **N**—Cathay Williams (11) **T**—Barak Obama (12) **U**—Nat Turner (13) **Y**—Sidney Poitier (14) **L**—Mae Jemison (15) **M**—Cudjoe Lewis (16) **I**—Benjamin Banneker (17) **C**—Sojourner Truth (18) **A**—Frederick Douglass (19) **Z**—Amos Fortune (20) **H**—Crispus Attucks (21) **X**—Langston Hughes (22) **J**—Fannie Lou Hamer (23) **B**—Martin Luther King, Jr. (24) **O**—Gwendolyn Brooks (25) **V**—Ida B. Wells (26) **E**—Dred Scott

Q/A #2. WHO SAID OR DID IT? –ANSWER KEY

Chapter One Answers: (1) Nana (Grandmother) (2) Kenyatta (3) Umama (Mother) (4) Matawan and Kenyatta (5) Nana (Grandmother) and Kenyatta (6) Utata (Father) (7) Kozo

Chapter Two Answers: (1) Kenyatta (2) The Captain (3) The enslaved children on the ship and Kenyatta (4) Kenyatta (5) Older enslaved gentleman on the ship (6) Nana Tala

Chapter Three Answers: (1) Enslaved children and Kenyatta (2) Nana Tala (3) Master Ames (4) Umama Sallie (5) Enslaved children at Ames Plantation (6) Kenyatta and Kozo

Chapter Four Answers: (1) Nana Tala (2) Kozo (3) Nana Tala (4) Young woman in the village (5) Nana (Kenyatta's Grandmother (6) Utata (Kenyatta's father)

Q/A #3. TERMS ANSWER KEY: (1) F (2) A (3) G (4) E (5) F (6) D (7) C (8) B

Q/A #4. YOUR TURN AFRICAN WORDS PARAGRAPH REWRITE:

My **Nana** Lily and **Nana** Henry live in Utah. I am their **abofra**, Shay. I live in Iowa with my **umama** and

utata and with my **onuabaa** Tara and **onuabarima** Jordon. My Uncle James and his **oyere** live next door.

Q/A #5. NAME WHERE IT HAPPENED ANSWER KEY—AFRICA or AMERICA? (1) America (2) Africa (3) Africa (4) America (5) Africa (6) America (7) Africa (8) America (9) America (10) America (11)

America (12) Africa (13) America (14) Africa (15) Africa (16) Africa (17) Africa (18) America (19) Africa (20) America

Q/A #6. MULTIPLE CHOICE ANSWER KEY: (1) B (2) B (3) B (4) A (5) B (6) B (7) B (8) B (9) A (10) B (11) A (12) A

Q/A #7. TRUE OR FALSE ANSWER KEY: (1). T (2) F (3) F (4) F (5) F (6) F (7) (8) F (9) F (10)T (11) T (12) F (13) F (14) F (15) T (16) F (17) T (18) F (19) F (20) T

Q/A #8. WORD SCRAMBLE ANSWER KEY: (1) Education (2) Freedom (3) Auction Block (4) Ship (5) Capture (6) Voyage (7) Chains (8) Family (9) Escape 10) Brave10

Q/A #10. YOUNGER STUDENTS RANDOM WORD LIST ACTIVITY: Column 1) Tree, Dog, School, Cry, Hot, Sea. Column 2) Smile, Sleep, Pot, Run.

Q/A #12. WORD SCRAMBLE YOUNGER STUDENTS:

SCRAMBLE 1. SOUP, SEA, TAIL, FREE, CRY

SCRAMBLE 2. SCHOOL, STONE, RUN, DOG

SCRAMBLE 3. WAG, HUT, MAT, FLUTE, HAPPY

SCRAMBLE 4. SHIP, TREE, POT, SLEEP, LAP

TERMS TO KNOW ANSWER KEY: (1) 12 (2) 5 (3) 1 (4) 3 (5) 11 (6) 10 (7) 16 (8) 13 (9) 2 (10) 6 (11) 17 (12) 4 (13) 8 (14) 15 (15) 9 (16) 14 (17) 7

OVERVIEW OF SLAVERY ANSWERS AND EXPLANATIONS:

1. **What is Enslavement**? It means being owned by another person and not being treated as a human being but as property. Enslaved persons are forced to work for another, and have no rights about where they live, what and when they eat and what they do. It means that they are not free to make their own decisions about their life, or move or go where they want to go, or say what they think. They are not allowed to get an education, get married (in most cases), or stay with their family in many instances. Being enslaved means a person cannot have their own home or land, choose the job they want, or take a break if they get tired or quit a job they dislike.
Source: kids.britannica.com

2. **Treatment of Slaves:** The enslaved were subjected to violence, beatings, separation from family and years of hardship. They were kidnapped from Africa and forced to work on plantations, in homes, farms, fields. For trying to escape, if caught, the enslaved could be severely punished or sold to another owner.
Source: "Colonial America Slavery, Middle Passage," ducksters.com

3. **From what regions of Africa were the enslaved taken?** Mostly West and Central regions of Africa and places such as Angola, Benin, Democratic Republic of Congo, Cameroon, Gabon, Gambia, Ghana, Guinea-Bissau, the Ivory Coast, Mali, Nigeria, Senegal were a few.
Source: history.com; kids.britannica.com

4. **How were the enslaved treated upon being captured and on their voyages on slave ships?** The enslaved were taken from their homeland, harshly treated, and chained around the neck, arms, and ankles. Some of the enslaved had also been enslaved in Africa, others were kidnapped. Those taken from Africa to America had to walk hundreds of miles to slave ships. Slave ships were fraught with disease, illness, pain, brutality, and sorrow. Captives were placed next to each other with no room to turn. Some of the enslaved died in what is called the "Middle Passage," which was part of the voyage across the Atlantic Ocean from Africa to the Americas.
Source: "Middle Passage," kidsbritannica.com

5. **What year did the enslavement of African/African Americans start in America and when did it end?** In 1619, the *White Lion,* an English ship sailed into the James River in Virginia carrying about 20 Africans on board, which is considered the beginning of the slave trade in America. **End of Slavery:** In January 1863, President Abraham Lincoln signed the Emancipation Proclamation freeing the enslaved. However those who were enslaved in Texas did not get word that they were free until June 19, 1865. The Thirteenth Amendment officially abolished slavery in the United States in 1865. One of the events that preceded slavery's final ending was the Civil War, and the loss of the South to the North.
Source: wikipedia.org; britannica.com

6. **How many Africans were brought to America and how many enslaved were in America in 1860?** The number of those brought from Africa in the beginning of the slave trade was slightly under 400,000. By 1860 the number of enslaved had reached nearly four million, with more than half living in the South.
Source: history.com

7. **Why was there Slavery in America?** The enslaved were used to farm, run households, and help the American economy grow. It was enslaved people of African descent that built some of America's most important buildings, universities, and the White House and Capital Buildings in Washington, DC. In the beginning of America's founding, Native Americans (some who were enslaved) and indentured slaves, who were Europeans who were poor, worked the land, and did other arduous and menial tasks, before the enslaved were imported from Africa as chattel in 1619.

Facts About Slavery

  o Large numbers of forced, free slave labor was relied upon to produce, harvest and pick crops such as cotton, tobacco, and other items which were profitable to the region.

  o The invention of the cotton gin accelerated the use of more and more enslaved to produce a profit.

  o Slavery was embraced in both the North and South in the early founding of the United States. All thirteen colonies allowed slavery.

  o It was the North that began to end slavery, an effort that was promoted by free blacks in the North and white and black abolitionists.

  o Not all Northerners were against the institution of slavery. Some were, however; against it.

o   Not all Southerners owned slaves, but the South greatly depended on free forced labor to maintain their economy and way of life.

   Source: "Colonial America," ducksters.com; "New England Colonies' Use of Slavery and Origins of Slavery," nationalgeographic.org

8. **Why were most of those enslaved in America of African descent?**

o   Indentured slaves were Europeans who had seven-year contracts in which they were paid for their labor and could leave their enslavement after completing their agreement.

o   Native Americans, who had been enslaved, knew the land, and could escape enslavement. Also it was reported that they fell ill to European diseases, brought over from the British colonists who came to America to gain independence from the King of England.

o   "The basis for African enslavement is that it was easier to import African slaves than it was to import slaves from other continents. Another reason Africans were enslaved is because unlike Native Americans, Africans were unfamiliar with America and did not know the land well enough to escape in masse. This fact was believed to prevent them from resisting, revolting, or escaping, but many did resist and fought for their freedom.

o   The natural talents of many Africans met the needs of the colonists. Africans, unlike some of the colonists, were experienced in agriculture, livestock and raising crops. The colonists quickly became dependent on the forced free labor of African slaves to do massive amounts of work to build the economic wealth of the North but mostly South.

o   Race. There was the belief that those of African descent were inferior to their owners and masters and were just property who were treated like animals. Their race and skin color also played a role in easily identifying the enslaved and keeping them in bondage.

9. **Which of the 13 American colonies allowed slavery?** All thirteen colonies allowed slavery in the beginning. However, by 1804, most northern states abolished or began the process of abolishing slavery. **Source:** www.mapsoftheworld.com

10. **Were there any U.S. presidents who owned slaves?** Yes. Twelve US Presidents owned the enslaved. George Washington, Thomas Jefferson, James Madison, James Monroe, Andrew Jackson, Martin Van Buren, William Henry Harrison, John Tyler, James K. Polk, Zachary Taylor, Andrew Johnson, and Ulysses S. Grant. **Source:** wikipedia.org; www.whitehousehistory.org

11. **What was the Declaration of Independence and why didn't it apply to the enslaved?** The document was created to declare that the United States of America was free and independent from England, and that it was a nation created with its own laws, which were established in the United States Constitution. While trying to form the United States in 1776, slavery was still occurring, more so in the South. To keep southern states from banding together and creating another nation of their own, the framers of the Constitution avoided offending the South by not opposing or addressing the issue of slavery because they needed their support to form what would become the United States.

   Source: "Thomas Jefferson: Liberty & Slavery", www.monticello.org; "Slavery: The Horrifying Institution," www.ushistory.org

12. **What were some of the tasks and chores the enslaved were forced to do?** The enslaved had numerous tasks, which may have included, depending on the slave owner, taking care of the household, catering to the slave owners and the slave owners children. Cooking, cleaning, sewing, washing clothes, and watching over enslaved children. The enslaved also built and maintained the plantation, picked crops, like cotton, and tobacco, cleared and plowed fields, planted seeds, tended to the animals, built structures such as sheds, houses, buildings. They also did additional labor of constructing plantations, universities, the White House and Nation's Capital Building. They laid tracks for railroads and crafted and made furniture and more. Basically, the enslaved did anything that was demanded of them. **Source:** khanacademy.com; wikipedia.org; history.com

13. **Were the enslaved separated from their families?** "Historian Michael Tadman has estimated that approximately one-third of enslaved children in the upper South states of Maryland and Virginia experienced family separation in one of three possible scenarios:

   o   Sold away from parents
   o   Sols with mother away from father
   o   Sold of mother or father away from child.

The fear of separation haunted adults who knew how likely it was to happen. Young children, innocently unaware of the possibilities, learned quickly of the pain that such separations could cost."
Source: "How Slavery Affected African American Families," nationalhumanitiescenter.org

14. **Why were the enslaved forbidden from going to school?** Some slave owners believed that if slaves were educated, they would revolt against being enslaved in great numbers, which would end the Souths' dependence on forced, free labor to maintain their economy. So, many states banned the education of people of African descent. They didn't want them to read about freedom and the Underground Railroad, or anything that was negative about slavery which might cause them to try to escape or rebel for a better life.
Source: wikipedia.org; www.spartacus-educational.com

15. **What type of foods were slaves given to eat?** It varied from meat, table scraps, cornmeal, fish, stews, soup whatever they could salvage. Some food was rationed and many of the enslaved nearly starved. Some grew their own gardens, if permitted to do so. In a slave narrative, one of the formerly enslaved women stated that some of the children's food was thrown in a pig trough and the enslaved children ate from there. Many slaves were hungry and restricted to very little food.
Source: wikipedia.org

16. **Did the enslaved attempt to escape or protest being enslaved?** Yes. From the beginning of their capture and enslavement, it is true that the enslaved were not "happy" or "joyous" about being enslaved. Even though there are books and movies that made it seem like the enslaved were pleased about working in the fields, farms, homes, and plantations, that was not the truth. They were not better off being enslaved. They had hearts, minds, feelings, talents, and dreams of freedom, like Kenyatta who stated, being enslaved meant, "No freedom to roam."

   o   Some of the enslaved, held up the work, and did other things to show that they were against being treated as property. Some of the enslaved even went to court to become free with the help of abolitionists who were White and also Black free men and women, or those who were former enslaved individuals.

o The most well-known rebellion against enslavement was led by Nat Turner in 1831. Also, abolitionists such as John Brown led a fiery revolt against slavery in 1859 in Harpers Ferry, West Virginia.

o According to Harvard professor and historian, Henry Louis Gates Jr., there were more than 200 revolts. The numbers of the enslaved, who tried to escape or run away on their own, numbered in the tens of thousands by the Civil War. Some of those seeking freedom stayed in Native American communities to try to avoid being caught.

o Abolitionists, as part of the Underground Railroad, aided those who were enslaved and seeking to escape to free states in the North and Canada. It was an elaborate system of "safe" homes, barns and places were the enslaved could stowaway and gain route information, momentary refuge, food, and support on their journey to freedom. Harriet Tubman was the main conductor who brought at least 300 of the enslaved to freedom.

Source: "Did African American Slaves Rebel?" by Henry Louis Gates, Jr., *pbs.org;* "Slave Resistance, Freedom's Story," nationalhumanitiescenter.org

17. **Why did some states do away with slavery?** There were individuals who were opposed to slavery due to religious beliefs and thought that it was wrong for humans to own humans and treat others like property, denying them equal rights. Abolitionists and free African Americans, on the behalf of the enslaved were filing court papers to gain freedom and arguing against the inhumanity of slavery. Others believed that it was not profitable to keep slavery in the North. **Source:** "How Did Slavery Disappear in the North?" abolitionseminar.org; "Vermont 1777: Early Steps Against Slavery," nmaahc.si.edu; "Freedom and Emancipation a Historical Overview," by Nicholas Boston and Jennifer Hallam, thirteen.org; "Becoming the Free North," nationalgeographic.org.

18. **What were free and slave states?** At the start of the Civil war more than thirty states made up the United States of America. Free states did not allow slavery, whereas slave states, did allow slavery. Some states that are now a part of the United States, were not yet founded at the time of the Civil War. (See information about free and slave states below).

    As of 1860 Free States: California, Connecticut, Illinois, Indiana, Iowa, Kansas, Maine, Massachusetts, Michigan, Minnesota, New York, Nevada, New Hampshire, New Jersey, Ohio, Oregon, Pennsylvania, Rhode Island, Wisconsin, Vermont.

    As of 1860 Slave States: Alabama, Arkansas, Delaware, Georgia, Florida, Kentucky, Louisiana, Maryland, Mississippi, Missouri, North Carolina, South Carolina, Tennessee, Texas, West Virginia, Virginia. **Source:** Slave States—worldpopulationreview.com (website that covers which states were free and slave states and the 1860 US Census).

19. **What was the Civil War, and Did it End Slavery?** Known as the only war within the United States, or the "War between the States," the North and South went to battle from April 12, 1861-April 9,1865 because the South was in favor of keeping slavery for their economic livelihoods. They threatened to secede or, (part), from mainly the Northern States to form their own Union if slavery were to be abolished. Several Southern States did secede, (left), to form the Confederacy. The war was instrumental in ending the battle between the states when the South was defeated. Presidential and legislative acts which included the signing the Emancipation Proclamation in 1863, by President Abraham Lincoln, which freed the enslaved and the Thirteenth Amendment, an act abolishing slavery in 1865, were also critical to ending forced slavery in the United States.

Source: "The American Civil War for Kids," ducksters.com; *The Causes of the Civil War* (video, ducksters.com)

20. **Did those who were enslaved fight in the Civil War?** Yes. Black men, both free and runaway enslaved, fought with the Union Army, (North), to end slavery forever. Black men made an impact in minor and major battles during the war and 10,000 men lost their lives. The Confederacy, (South), had established laws barring Black men from serving as combat troops or bearing arms, (having guns). A month or so before the end of the Civil War the Confederate Congress agreed to allow black men to serve as combat troops; however, they would still be enslaved. According to military records, no Black men actually fought for the Southern cause.
Source: wikipedia.org, "*Black Confederate Battlefields: Truth and Legend,*" by Sam Smith, American Battlefield Trust.

21. **What is the Emancipation Proclamation?** President Abraham Lincoln wanted to keep both the North and South together, as one nation. The issue of slavery was dividing the nation. On January 3, 1863, President Lincoln signed the Emancipation Proclamation freeing the enslaved; however, the enslaved in Texas didn't learn of the news until June 1865. Despite Lincoln signing the Emancipation Proclamation, the Civil War continued until the South surrendered in April 1865.
Source: ducksters.com; kids.britannica.com

22. **What is Juneteenth and Why is it Celebrated in the African American Community?** Word of the Emancipation Proclamation freeing slaves did not reach the state of Texas until June 19, 1865. When it did, that day became known as Juneteenth, which was recognition of true freedom for African Americans. Since June 19, 1866, the day has been recognized as the true freedom or independence day for people of African descent. When the 4th of July was first celebrated in the United States and for many years afterward, not all African Americans were free or even considered American citizens.
Source: wikipedia.org; history.com; "The Historical Legacy of Juneteenth," nmaahc.si.edu

23. **What are the Thirteenth, Fourteenth and Fifteenth Amendments?** Three Amendments that pertained to important rights that were denied African Americans were established as a part of the United States Constitution. The 13th Amendment abolished slavery. The 14th Amendment granted citizenship and civil rights to the formerly enslaved and the 15th Amendment granted African American men the right to vote.
Source: ducksters.com; nationalgeograhic.org

24. **What happened to the newly freed enslaved after the Civil War and the end of slavery?** Some made an exodus to other states like Kansas to escape the oppression and violence of the South, while others had nowhere to go and stayed with their former owners and worked for wages. A Freedmen's Bureau was set up by the government to help poor Southerners and newly freed African Americans with the basics, such as food, shelter, medical care, and schooling, which many of the formerly enslaved took advantage of due to the years they were not permitted an opportunity to learn. The black church also rose to be a major center of the community of the formerly enslaved. African American men became an important part of the United Congress during the period of Reconstruction.
Source: "The African American Odyssey: A Quest for Full Citizenship," loc.gov

What was the Reconstruction Era? The period after slavery was known as the Reconstruction Era (1865-1877). It was the time that the South, which was destroyed after the war, was rebuilt and states that seceded, or left, rejoined the Union. Some of the formerly enslaved people of African descent were to be included in American Society, and granted rights by the passage of the 13th, 14th and 15th Amendments. During Reconstruction, some formerly enslaved individuals were a part of the United States Congress and the Senate and made other gains, but for the most part they faced hardship. After President Lincoln was assassinated by John Wilkes Booth in April 1865, his successor, President Andrew Johnson broke the promise to improve the lives of the enslaved and never fulfilled a promise that would assure the former enslaved 40 acres of land and a mule to help them get established.

VIOLENCE AGAINST AFRICAN AMERICANS

By 1865, the Ku Klux Klan, which is often referred to as the KKK, were prominent. They wore white hoods and robes, and continually terrorized African Americans across the country. They existed mostly in the South and were against African Americans having rights, and they also targeted other racial and religious groups. By 1877 Southern States established Black Codes to reverse and restrict the gains of African Americans that were granted after slavery was abolished. **Source:** senate.gov; "American Civil War, Civil War Reconstruction," ducksters.com; "Reconstruction Era Facts for Kids," historyforkids.org; Ku Klux Klan, kids.britannica.com; Reconstruction Amendments, kids.kiddle.com

SLAVERY TIMELINE IN AMERICA THROUGH THE CIVIL RIGHTS MOVEMENT (An abbreviated history). This timeline reflects some of the major laws, and legislative acts pertaining to African and African Americans in the United States.

1619 August — About twenty Africans, were seized from a Portuguese slave ship, and were forcibly taken to Jamestown, Virginia, and traded for provisions. They were classified as indentured servants.

1640 July 9 — When three runaway indentured servants were captured, the General Court of Colonial Virginia gave the indentured slaves additional years to serve while John Punch, a black man, was sentenced to servitude for life. Punch was the first African in Virginia to be enslaved for life."

1641 — Massachusetts became the first North American colony to recognize slavery as a legal institution.

1662-1663 — A Virginia law, passed in 1662, determined that if a mother was enslaved, her child would be enslaved too. More restrictive laws were passed which resulted in the Virginia Slave Codes of 1705.

1676 — Bacon's Rebellion in Virginia included poor white and black people who fought together against being enslaved, leading the government to establish laws to quickly embrace enslaving people of African descent.

1688 — Pennsylvania Quakers adopted the first formal anti-slavery resolution in American History.

1705 – The Virginia Slave Code further limited the freedom of the enslaved and defined some rights of slave owners. It also allowed slave owners to punish slaves without fear of legal repercussions and specified the rewards for the recapture of runaway slaves.

1712 April — A slave revolt in New York City, led to increased restrictions on slaves.

1770 March 5 — Crispus Attucks, was an ex-slave, and one of the first to die while fighting against the British in the American Revolution. The event later became known as the Boston Massacre.

1775 April 14 — The Pennsylvania Society for the Abolition of Slavery was founded.

1775 December 30 — General George Washington ordered recruiting officers to accept free black individuals in the American Army where they had once been banned from serving. More than 5,000 black individuals, mostly Northerners, fought against the British.

1776 July 4 — The Continental Congress adopted the *Declaration of Independence. However, the enslaved and even some free people of African Descent were excluded from the ideals expressed in the Declaration of Independence, which was the critical document in which America was founded.

1780 — Gradual Emancipation Act was passed in Pennsylvania.

1783 — The American Revolution ends.

1793 February 12 — Congress passed the first Fugitive Slave Act, making it a crime to harbor an escaped slave or to interfere with the arrest of a slave.

Early 1800s. Westward expansion, along with a growing abolition movement in the North, sparks a national debate over slavery. Southern states want new territories in the West to become slave-holding states.

1800s — Anti-slavery Northerners helped slaves escape from southern plantations to the North via a loose network of safe houses called **the Underground Railroad**.

1807 — Thomas Jefferson signed Act prohibiting importation of slaves.

1808 January 1 — Laws banning the African slave trade went into effect in the United States and in all British Colonies.

1816 April 9 — The African Methodist Episcopal Church, the first all-black religious denomination in the United States, was formally organized, and Richard Allen was named its first bishop.

1816 December 28 — The American Colonization Society was founded to transport freeborn blacks and emancipated slaves to Africa, leading to the creation of a colony in 1824, that became the Republic of Liberia in 1847.

1820 March 3 — The Missouri Compromise was approved by Congress. Missouri was admitted to the Union as a slave state, Maine entered as a free state, and slavery was prohibited in western territories north of Missouri's southern border.

1831 August 21-22 — Nat Turner led a slave revolt. The **American Anti-Slavery Society** is founded.

1839 — A slave revolt aboard the *Amistad* resulted in the 1841 United States Supreme Court decision affirming that the African captives were free individuals with the right to resist "unlawful" slavery.

1845 — Frederick Douglass publishes his first autobiography and best-known work, *Narrative of the Life of Frederick Douglass, an American Slave.*

1850 — The Compromise of 1850 brought California into the United States as a free state, banned public sale of slaves in the District of Columbia, opened up the rest of the lands seized from Mexico to settlement by slave owners, and committed the United States government to enforcement of a new fugitive slave law."

1852 March 20 — The anti-slavery novel *Uncle Tom's Cabin*, written by Harriet Beecher Stowe was published, and, by year's end, 300,000 copies were sold in the United States. *Tom Shows,* dramatizations based on the plot of the novel, were widely performed by traveling companies into the 20th century, spreading common stereotypes of African Americans.

1854 — The Kansas-Nebraska Act mandated that a popular vote of the settlers would determine if territories became free or slave states. The newly formed Republican Party vowed to prevent new slave states and quickly became the majority party in nearly every northern state."

1857 March 6 — In Dred Scott v. Sandford, the United States Supreme Court ruled that black people were not citizens of the United States and denied Congress the ability to prohibit slavery in any federal territory.

1859 — John Brown, an abolitionist, raided Harper's Ferry in attempt to free the enslaved.

1860-1861 — Abraham Lincoln was elected President of the United States, the southern states seceded, and the United States Civil War began. The 1860 census showed the black population of the United States to be 4,441,830, of which 3,953,760 were enslaved and 488,070 were free."

1863 January 1, 1863 — President Abraham Lincoln signed the Emancipation Proclamation, freeing all enslaved people of African Descent except those in Texas who were unaware until 1865, that they were also freed.

1865 — The Thirteenth Amendment is passed abolishing slavery in the United States.

1865 — June 19, 1865 — Was the beginning of what came to be known as Juneteenth. In the state of Texas more than 200,000 enslaved were informed they were free.

1865 — The state of Mississippi is the first to impose Black Codes, after the Civil War, which discriminates and restricts rights of free African Americans.

1868 — The Fourteenth Amendment is passed and grants citizenship rights and equal protection under the law to formerly enslaved African Americans.

1870 — The 15th Amendment was enacted giving the right to vote to African American men.

1865-1877 — Reconstruction Era, was the time after slavery. There was the establishment of Freedmen's Bureau, which helped with establishing schools and other organizations to help the former enslaved with their new lives.

1885 — Many Southern States passed laws to keep White and Black students from attending school together.

1954 — Brown vs. the Board of Education. The United States Supreme Court ordered public schools to integrate.

1955-1968 — The Civil Rights Movement was born, which was a period that African Americans pushed to be treated as human beings, and not second-class citizens. They sought equal rights in the United States which would entitle them the right to vote, access to equal education, fair housing, jobs, and all of the rights that they were denied based on race and ethnic background. Some of their efforts to be free and equal led to acts of brutality against them.

1963 — March on Washington for Jobs and Freedom. Dr. Martin Luther King, Jr. gave his famous "I Have a Dream" speech 100 years after Abraham Lincoln signed the Emancipation Proclamation.

1964 — Passage of the Civil Rights Act of 1964 prohibited discrimination in employment based on race, color, religion, national origin, and gender in public accommodations, employment, and federally funded programs.

1965 — Voting Rights Act — Major legislation signed by President Lyndon B. Johnson prohibited racial discrimination in voting.

1968 — Fair Housing Act — Prohibited discrimination in housing based on race, religion, and national origin.

1968 — Martin Luther King Jr., the most well-known civil rights activist, is killed in Memphis, Tennessee on April 4, 1968.

Sources: wikipedia.org; Ferris University — Jim Crow Museum, ushistory.org, theguardian.com; history.com, infoplease.com; Monet Hendricks: African American Timeline, socialstudies.com

Today — Despite the end of slavery and the passage of the 13th, 14th and 15th amendments, African Americans still encounter discrimination and acts of violence based on race. After slavery ended, many Southern States adopted "Jim Crow" laws throughout the years that separated white and black individuals by race, (a practice known as segregation), on public forms of transportation, including buses, trains, street cars and even some airlines. These restrictions even extended to marriage between the races. People of African descent were restricted from many neighborhoods, public swimming pools, hospitals, libraries, schools, hotels, theaters, restaurants, and other establishments. In addition, certain areas of life, such as employment, education, voting rights and housing were not equal or fair to people of African descent.

 In time, many advances and gains for African Americans and other Americans occurred through civil rights legislation that was pushed forward by the brave and courageous efforts of Dr. Martin Luther King, Jr. and other valiant civil rights advocates, as well as people of all races who had the desire to work together for change in America. Many lost their lives throughout the decades in the fight for dignity and freedom for all. Still, however, despite positive changes, the fight for equality and justice continues.

About the Author — Joslyn Gaines Vanderpool is a writer, motivational speaker, and empowerment specialist who lives in Northern California with her husband and daughter. She attained a bachelor's degree in Political Science from the University of California, Berkeley. Over the years, she has had a varied career that involved working as a congressional intern, writer and editor for political and urban magazines, and years of service in the field of education at Howard University, the University of New Mexico, and American River College. Joslyn encourages others to pursue their passions, attain their dreams, recognize their own value and the value and beauty in others.

As a citizen of the world, Joslyn has traveled and met people from all regions of the globe through her work activities and personal journeys. She has been a guest lecturer in college Minority in America classes where she has spoken about women's issues and the African American experience.

About the Illustrator—Sacramento based artist Beau Allen has been honing his skills in illustration art for the past few years. Originally a portrait artist, Beau combined his creative skill with his love for continued learning, blending his natural talents and formal education, bringing about the perfect fusion of his two passions.

Beau's evolution into illustration art allowed him to introduce another element into this union and extend the range of his artistry, utilizing facial expressions to tell and enhance a writer's narrative, further connecting the reader to explore the depths of story and connect to the characters' experiences.

About the Author — Joslyn Gaines Vanderpool is a writer, motivational speaker, and empowerment specialist who lives in Northern California with her husband and daughter. She attained a bachelor's degree in political science from the University of California, Berkeley. Over the years, she has had a varied career that involved working as a congressional intern, writer and editor for political and urban magazines, and years of service in the field of education at Howard University, the University of New Mexico, and American River College. Joslyn encourages others to pursue their passions, attain their dreams, recognize their own value and the value and beauty in others.

As a citizen of the world, Joslyn has traveled and met people from all regions of the globe through her work activities and personal journeys. She has been a guest lecturer in college Minority in America classes where she has spoken about women's issues and the African American experience.

About the Illustrator—Sacramento based artist Beau Allen has been honing his skills in illustration art for the past few years. Originally a portrait artist, Beau combined his creative skill with his love for continued learning, blending his natural talents and formal education, bringing about the perfect fusion of his two passions.

Beau's evolution into illustration art allowed him to introduce another element into this union and extend the range of his artistry, utilizing facial expressions to tell and enhance a writer's narrative, further connecting the reader to explore the depths of story and connect to the characters' experiences.

9 781941 859889